Robert's Rules of Order

A Complete Guide to Robert's Rules of Order

Table of Contents

Introduction 1

Chapter 1 – An Overview of Robert's Rules of Order 2

Chapter 2 – History of Robert's Rules of Order 10

Chapter 3 – Benefits of Using Robert's Rules of Order 13

Chapter 4 – When and How You Can Use the Rules 23

Chapter 5 – Key Terms and Scripts to be Aware of 28

Chapter 6 – How to Introduce the Rules to an Organization .. 53

Chapter 7 – Important Governing Documents 58

Chapter 8 – Using Minutes in Your Meetings 91

Chapter 9 – Frequently Asked Questions 101

Conclusion 122

Introduction

Thanks for taking the time to read this book on Robert's Rules of Order.

This book aims to serve as a comprehensive guide to parliamentary procedures, as outlined in Robert's Rules of Order, and how to implement such rules and structure to your own organization.

Robert's Rules of Order have been used for decades to enhance the productivity and efficiency of meetings. In addition, the implementation of Robert's Rules of Order helps to ensure that fairness and democracy is ever-present in the organizations that choose to use this system.

Robert's Rules of Order are applicable to a huge variety of organizations. From small, community-led groups to large, publicly-traded companies, Robert's Rules has been used successfully by all matters of organizations for decades!

Once again, thanks for choosing this book. I hope you find it to be helpful!

Chapter 1 – An Overview of Robert's Rules of Order

Certain principles and procedures are considered universal when it comes to the process of making decisions. These may apply for simple personal matters, such as whenever your family is deciding on where to go for the upcoming holidays. A similar decision-making process can also be applied in a business or any organizational setting. For example, facilitating a meeting among the team members would require, at a certain point, for the group to come to an agreement on how to proceed regarding a particular issue.

The principles and procedures that are applied during these meetings are collectively known as parliamentary procedures. In the most basic sense, parliamentary procedures have been designed to govern how a decision will be made in any type of setting. By following the standards and guidelines stated in the parliamentary procedures, every party involved can expect that order and fairness will be upheld throughout the course of the process.

To ensure the proper implementation of parliamentary procedures, Robert's Rules of Order was written and presented as a manual of consolidated principles and processes. Due to the extensiveness of the topics covered, the manual has been recognized by a wide range of organizations and experts from different fields of interests.

Basic Elements of Robert's Rules of Order

Understanding how to use and apply the contents of the manual entails learning about its different parts. Robert's Rules of Order was designed as comprehensive guide for anyone who wishes to improve how their meetings are being run, and how decisions are being made by the group he or she belongs to.

Given its thoroughness, it can be daunting for beginners to navigate the manual, especially when they need to find a certain topic or standard that is applicable to their current situation.

As a prerequisite for the successful application of Robert's Rules of Order, it is necessary for all leaders and members of a group to have a copy of the manual. Hard copies are available in almost all libraries, as well as all major bookstores. If you would rather read an electronic copy of it, there are free online versions of the previous editions, which may also sufficiently serve as a reference while you are trying to master the parliamentary procedures.

Motions and Voting

There are several sections of the manual, but the most in-depth one is all about making motions during a meeting. There are four general types of motions that a member can execute depending on their intention:

- ***Main or Principal Motion***

    This pertains to a statement made by a member of the organization in order to propose an action or present an opinion for the evaluation and approval of the assembly.

    All main motions require a second before they can be opened up for debate. For it to be adopted, the motion must gain the majority vote, or the two-thirds vote, depending on what is stated in the organization's bylaws. Once it has been passed, the organization is allowed to propose amendments to the said motion, but these motions will have to go through the same process of review and approval.

When a member is making a main motion, no member is allowed to interrupt the one who has taken the floor. In order to prevent any confusion or miscommunication among the members of the assembly, it's best to include as many details as possible into the statement.

- ***Privileged Motions***

  The main point of privileged motions is to get the attention of the assembly on matters that concern the rights of the members. Even if there is an ongoing or pending discussion, debate, or vote, a privileged motion will take precedence over any other motion that has been made and recognized by the assembly.

  Common examples include the motion to take a recess from the meeting, and to call for the orders of the day, which is made whenever there is a need to realign the focus of the members on the agenda of the current meeting.

- ***Incidental Motions***

  These motions are made depending on what business is being discussed at that given time. For example, a motion to appeal the ruling of the chair may be made by a member in reaction to the decisions of the chairperson regarding a previously made motion.

  This is different from an incidental main motion, which can only be made when there is no other pending business left on the agenda of the meeting. It cannot, however, bring new business to the attention of the assembly. Incidental main motions can only qualify or modify the business that has already been brought forward to the attention of the assembly. When this type of motion is made and recognized, it will be treated similarly to a main motion.

- *Subsidiary*

    In the case that a main motion has to be disposed of, a subsidiary motion may be made by any member of the assembly. Because of this, such motions have to take precedence over the other types, except for privileged motions made around the same time.

    A common example of a subsidiary motion is a motion to refer the motion to a committee, which would direct a subset of the members to evaluate the motion first, before it can be voted upon by the rest of the assembly.

It is important for everyone in the group to understand the differences between each type of motion, and which one will take precedence over the others in various types of situations. There are also rules when it comes to making motions, seconding motions, and arriving at resolutions. At the end of it, a series of steps must then be followed in order to take the motion to a vote.

In most cases, motions are easily decided upon by the group. However, no matter how cohesive the group is, there are instances wherein a certain motion might trigger a debate among the members before a vote can be taken.

Handling, resolving, and preventing debates about a motion are also discussed in Robert's Rules of Order.

Included in the manual as well are the circumstances wherein a motion can be exempted from a debate. For example, there are people who are incredibly passionate about their beliefs and points of view, and such intensity could sometimes lead them into making the debate personal rather than objective.

Aside from debates, people also have a tendency to break the social order whenever they get carried away by their thoughts. Robert's Rules of Order emphasizes the role of the chair in clarifying that whoever is making a motion has the floor at the moment, and any possible interruption is not allowed unless the chair recognizes the need for it.

There are plenty more rules relating to meeting decorum discussed in the manual, all of which are important in maintaining and putting order back into the meeting whenever necessary.

When it comes to voting, Robert's Rules of Order has also specified the proper means of asking the group if all members are ready for a vote. If they are, the manual also explicitly states the manner on how to formally announce a vote during a meeting. In most cases, gaining the majority vote will decide the final resolution about the motion. However, the manual is careful enough to explain certain instances wherein some votes can be nullified even though everyone is in agreement about their decision or their next course of action.

Committees and Boards

Another section in the manual discusses the proper way to classify committees, and all the applicable rules that will govern each class. Committees may be formed within a group according to these five primary classifications:

- *General Committee*

    This committee is typically established in the bylaws, but it may also be created later depending on the current requirements of the organization. This is composed of the members who are present for the given meeting instead of the entire membership.

    The main objective of the general committee is to resolve and close the businesses identified in the agenda, so long as such items will not create a significant impact or change in the organization as a whole. During this time, the rules are usually less stringent, so as to better facilitate the actions and decisions of the general committee.

- *Standing Committee*

    A standing committee may only be established if the bylaws have specified the need for such a committee to exist within the organization. They serve a regular function and therefore are considered permanent, unless the bylaws have been duly amended.

    Common examples of standing committees include the nominating committee which is responsible for proposing a slate of candidates for the consideration of the board and the assembly, and the finance and budget committee, which handles all processes and obligations pertaining to the financial aspects of the organization.

- *Special or Ad Hoc Committee*

    To form a special committee, a member must make a motion to create one, and the assembly must then vote in favor of the said motion. The primary objective of a special committee must be stated in the motion since it has to be specific and has not been covered by the responsibilities of the standing committee.

A special committee may only last until the given task or responsibility has been completed. After that, the members must make their report and present it to the chair and the assembly.

- ***Executive Committee***

    The board of directors or trustees belong to the executive committee of a given organization. This is a small group that has either been elected or appointed to make decisions for the organization. The level of their power, however, is defined in the bylaws in order to establish a check-and-balance system between them and the members of the organization.

Nominations and Elections

The corresponding roles and responsibilities of each officer assigned within a committee are also described in Robert's Rules of Order. It is important to note, however, that these descriptions are not set in stone. An organization may alter them according to their needs and what is stated in their own bylaws.

In addition, even though Robert's Rules of Order specifies the protocol that must be followed during the nominations and elections of officers, the responsibility of formalizing the policies pertaining to these matters is assigned to the board. This means that the manual serves as the foundation upon which the organizational policies are built.

Any deviations, unusual cases, and other important issues that may be encountered during the nomination and election process are also addressed by Robert's Rules of Order. Because of these inclusions, the manual is regarded as an incredibly valuable resource for many organizations today and in the years to come.

Robert's Rules of Order is a manual designed to help organizations apply parliamentary procedures in a democratic manner. Over the years, practitioners have found several ways to modify its principles and rules, while still preserving the original intentions of its author. Such developments have allowed Robert's Rules of Order to become a universal system that can cross borders and withstand the changes brought about by time.

Chapter 2 – History of Robert's Rules of Order

Before delving into the specifics of the manual, the best way to begin understanding a concept is by first learning its history. It is important to consider what the original intentions of its creator were and take into consideration how it has evolved since its first incarnation. From there, you can gain a more rounded understanding of how you can apply the principles and procedures stated in the manual.

A common misconception about Robert's Rule of Order is that, due to its nature, a lawyer or a judge must have written and presented the first version of the manual. However, Henry Martyn Robert, the original author, was neither of those things. But he did have the skills and expertise to design and consolidate the standards and practices of parliamentary procedure into a comprehensive reference material that would be applicable for any purpose.

Henry Martyn Robert was a career military man, gaining a rank of brigadier general by the end of his time in the United States Army. Academically speaking, he was trained as an engineer, and he even managed to apply his training when he was asked to improve the then-current waterway systems.

Given his achievements, he was well-regarded by his peers and the community, so, one day, he was asked to lead the town meeting at the local church. With his training and experience in the military, Robert had gained a slight familiarity with parliamentary procedures, but unfortunately, his knowledge ended there. At the time, he had no idea to how to apply the principles in facilitating a rather simple meeting. As a man of honor, however, he tried to do his best without the help of a guide book, relying solely on what little knowledge he had with him. The meeting was fairly well received, but as he left, Robert felt embarrassed about the insecurity and incompetence that he had displayed during the course of his performance as the facilitator.

Since he was considered a prominent member of their neighborhood, Robert would likely be invited once more to head and run meetings and other similar events. Fresh from his self-declared defeat, he resolved to prevent his mistakes from happening again in the future. First, he went out and gathered books about parliamentary procedures. As he studied them, he took notes before proceeding to his next step.

Robert then sought his comrades in the military to interview them about their respective opinions about parliamentary procedures. Based on his findings, he concluded that no two books or individuals offer the same understanding of the parliamentary procedures. Furthermore, due to the lack of uniformity, many who participated in meetings did not see the point of following the parliamentary procedures. Some even actively despised the concept due to the said inconsistencies in terms of its implementation.

The most important conclusion, however, is that even though the parliamentary procedures were widely questioned at the time, many would appreciate a definitive guide that could serve its purpose no matter who was reading it, or in which setting it would be used. Robert also determined that the best source of parliamentary procedures to document was the Congress itself. And so, he recorded each rule and current practice of the members of the Congress and applied their standards to the needs of other non-legislative organizations.

Gen. Robert dedicated months to completing his manual. Another challenge he faced at the time was finding and securing a publisher for his manuscript. Because of this, he opted to self-publish his work, then entitled as the "Pocket Manual of Rules of Order for Deliberative Assemblies". It was 176 pages long, and around 4,000 copies were printed at of Gen. Robert's expense.

From there, the relatively small launching of his book gained the attention of the general public. A publisher from Chicago named S. C. Griggs Company reached out to Gen. Robert with an offer to publish more copies of his manual. The publisher had also suggested a change of title, making it catchier and more concise - thus the creation of the first edition of Robert's Rules of Order.

The relaunching of the manual proved to be a great success for both the author and the publisher. The first batch of about 3,000 copies sold out within the first four months. Since that time, ten more updated versions of the manual have been published. In 1915 and 1970, significant revisions to the content were made.

Nowadays, Robert's Rules of Order is no longer the work of single man, but rather, a group of experts in parliamentary procedures who are all responsible for keeping the material relevant to its users. Copies are also made accessible to anybody who wishes to read the original edition, but the most recent version was published in 2011. Gen. Robert may have passed away in 1923, but his legacy and contribution to society remains accessible to anyone who is willing to abide by his manual.

Chapter 3 – Benefits of Using Robert's Rules of Order

Robert's Rules of Order is a collection of principles and processes that permits all members of an organization to conduct and manage their business and agenda in an efficient and orderly manner. Before the manual was first published, people simply referred to those processes and rules as parliamentary procedures. What Gen. Robert did was gather the best practices and policies, and document them in a detailed and systematic manner, making the manual readable and useable for anyone, in any type of organization.

Given this, the benefits of complying with the parliamentary procedures is equivalent - if not further enhanced - by following Robert's Rules of Order. Gen. Robert was also careful enough to ensure that the benefits of parliamentary procedures would not be lost in his own interpretation of the concept's guiding principles and rules. As such, his work is merely a reflection of the best version of the parliamentary procedures governing practitioners and organizations.

Even after the publication of the manual, people who were not familiar with parliamentary procedures would question why a rigid structure matters in their organization. Furthermore, it is common to hear questions about the differences and improvements that the parliamentary procedures could make.

To answer such queries, you may compare the knowledge of parliamentary procedures with the knowledge of the laws and rules involved when you are driving a vehicle. When you have studied completely the proper way of driving, you are less likely to be fined for violations of the law. More importantly, you would be less likely be involved in major or minor traffic accidents.

At the most basic level, you would know which side of the road you should be driving on - a simple yet variable factor depending on which country you are going to traverse in your vehicle. You would also know who has the right of way between two cars when trying to turn at or cross an intersection. When everyone knows and follows the exact laws of the land pertaining to driving and the road, the flow of the traffic will be smooth, and the likelihood of an accident will be significantly lessened.

Similarly, when every member of an organization is following the same set of rules when it comes to meetings, there is a higher chance that the proceedings will remain steady and smooth. Confrontations and conflicts between the members may also be avoided, especially during discussions of sensitive or controversial topics. Ultimately, following the parliamentary procedures can make the meetings held by your organization become more objective, without sacrificing productivity.

Guiding Principles of Robert's Rules of Order

At its core, the basic tenets of Robert's Rules of Order are as follows:

- There must be an individual assigned to direct the flow of discussion and facilitate the exchange of ideas, in order to ensure the order of the meeting.

- All individuals who are considered members of the group have the freedom to speak their thoughts, discuss their ideas with the other members and the facilitator, and arrive at their own conclusions.

- At the end of the discussion of ideas, there must be a consensus among the group on what will be next course of action about the opportunities and/or challenges that have been brought up by a member of the group.

- Members must understand and acknowledge that the majority rules. It should be noted, however, that there are mechanisms in place to protect the rights of the minority, thereby letting them speak their case, and to vote according to their views about the matter at hand.

Promoting these ideas over the years has helped small and large organizations alike. Members no longer have to guess or make up their own rules, which typically will lead them to conflict and disagreement with one another. The meetings following the standards set out in the manual are regarded as objective and systematic. As such, the group can focus more on being productive and rational, especially during the course of the meeting itself.

Specific Rules That Will Benefit Your Organization

You might be thinking that the general concepts given above may be achieved even without trying to learn and follow Robert's Rules of Order. However, why expend so much time and effort in coming up with your own rules when you can simply refer to this manual of standard parliamentary procedures?

Here are the various rules that constitute the principles guiding Robert's Rules of Order:

- *Going through your business one at a time*

    According to experts, multitasking isn't actually a good practice since it lessens the quality of output and, at times, may even cause unnecessary delay to the completion of a given task. Focus is key in achieving the correct output in the least amount of time. Because of this, the parliamentary procedures make it a point, through the following rules, to encourage its followers to handle a list of responsibilities one at a time:

a. Every meeting must have an agenda specifying the order of business that everyone must follow. Each item on the agenda is discussed and reviewed in the proper order, as specified in the agenda. Before moving on to the next matter, all members must agree that the current agenda has been resolved or disposed of accordingly.

b. There can be only one main motion at any given time. Upcoming motions will have to wait until the group has voted upon what should be done regarding the current main motion.

c. If there is pending motion, members can still make new motions as long as they are only secondary motions. In addition, when a secondary motion has been taken on by the group, it will be discussed first before tackling the main motion again. Examples of common secondary motions include the motion to amend and the motion to postpone.

d. There can only be one member taking the floor at any given time. This means that if a member wants to speak, they must formally make it known to the presiding officer. By doing so, everyone will be guaranteed a fair chance to speak their minds and make their case in front of the assembly.

e. Every member who wishes to speak will have to take turns. No individual is granted the privilege to speak solely for the entirety of the meeting. As specified in the parliamentary procedures, a meeting is a venue where an exchange of ideas among the members can take place.

f. Speaking twice about a motion is not allowable unless every member has had the chance to take the floor and speak. Through this, fairness and efficiency are ensured throughout the discussion.

- *Fostering a culture of justice, equality, courtesy, and objectivity*

    When we were children, our parents and teachers promoted the value of being respectful to the people around us. Carrying forward this value into adulthood is a great asset in maintaining peace and harmony, especially at an organizational level. As shown below, the parliamentary procedures are also developed and practiced as a means of preserving the high quality of relationships the members have with one another:

    a. For every meeting, the presiding officer or the chair has to start the meeting or call the meeting to order according to the time specified on the schedule of the meeting. This practice extends courtesy to the members who have already arrived for the meeting. It is also a way to show that everyone values the time of one another since the chair or presiding officer is not going to wait for the arrival of latecomers, no matter what their positions are or how significant they are to the meeting itself.

    b. After the meeting has been called to order, all members are expected to sit down in their respective seats. All unnecessary conversations between one another should also cease to give way to the next steps of the meeting.

    c. Members who have been assigned to present reports to the assembly must be seated up front. By doing so, the time it will take them to reach the microphone or podium will be lessened. They will also not end up disturbing the other members.

d. Speaking must be done in a clear and concise manner. The volume of the voice should be loud enough for everyone within the room to hear. To facilitate this, a microphone may be provided to the speaking member.

e. If an officer or member is speaking, everyone must take the time and effort to listen to what they have to say.

f. If a member wishes to be acknowledged by the presiding officer, he or she stands up without speaking a word. This will show your interest or need for attention, while still maintaining respectful behavior towards the person who is speaking at the time.

g. To preserve the expected social distance between the members, each individual refers to another person using the third person. If the said individual is an elected official, then you have to refer to them using the title of their given position.

For instance, you may refer to the chair as Mr. Chairman or Madam Chairman, depending on the person's gender. If the individual does not have any title, the third person must still be used to prevent the discussion from being personal or overly familiar. This also ensures that the chances of name-calling or personal insults to one another are significantly lessened among members.

h. When engaged in a debate, the members are not allowed to talk over one another, or even to talk directly to the other party or the listening members. Every remark made by a member has to be addressed to the presiding officer or chair.

i. During the course of a discussion, the members must remain on topic and speak only of their issues about the said topic, and not about their personal issues with other members. There should be no questions or remarks about the different personalities and motives of other members. The presiding officer is responsible for ensuring that all members are abiding by these rules for the entirety of the meeting.

j. If the presiding officer has a correction to make about a member's behavior or statement, the correction must not be made using the name of the member in question. For example, if a member is breaking the rule about making no personal attacks whatsoever against other members, the presiding officer may call his or her attention by referring to the member as the "speaker".

Another way of doing this is by pointing out that "the motion is out of order" instead of the saying directly that the member is out of order. If ever the presiding officer calls out a member by his or her name, it means that the member is being officially charged with an offense.

In terms of exhibiting equality, courtesy, and objectiveness during a meeting, here are the specific rules in the parliamentary procedures that you may apply within your organization:

a. During a debate, the presiding officer is not allowed to take sides, or show an inclination or preference for one side over the other. In case he or she has an opinion on the matter at hand, the chair - along with its responsibilities and privileges - will have to be fully relinquished by that person. He or she will only be allowed to make their case and vote upon their point of view about the given matter.

b. All sides of an issue must be heard, especially during a debate. Compliance with the rules of the debate is expected from all members. This includes listening well to the point being made by the opposing party, even if you have a counterargument already in mind.

c. All members and the presiding officer must know the rules of the organization and how to apply them judiciously in different situations. It is advisable to correct the major infractions committed by a member to another member or the presiding officer. A point of order should not be raised if the infraction is only minor, and the rights of the members are not being infringed upon.

d. If a topic has been deemed sensitive or controversial by the members, they have the right to make a motion for the voting to be done through the ballot system. The ballot ensures that the decisions made by members will remain private unless the member willingly discloses it. Since the vote is confidential, there is little to no chance that others might retaliate towards those who have voted differently.

e. When a member has been formally accused of a wrongdoing by the other members or the presiding officer, he or she has the right to undergo a trial instead of being charged immediately and without due process.

- *<u>Preserving the rule of the majority and protecting the rights of the minority</u>*

    Given that the majority rules in terms of parliamentary procedures, having the right to vote is one of the most essential rights possessed by all members of an organization. Even if they are in the majority, this does not mean that those members have the power to take away the rights of other members or silence the voice of the minority, including the absentees and the individual members. Such balance in the assembly can be established and sustained through the following rules:

a. Every member of an organization must be notified of the schedule and agenda of all meetings. This can be done through various channels of communication, including mail posts, telephone calls, emails, or a verbal announcement during or near the end of the previous meeting.

b. If an already adopted motion is going to be amended or rescinded, as proposed by a certain individual, all members must be notified before the proposal can be discussed and voted upon on during the next meeting.

c. During situations wherein the rights of the members might be taken away from them, a majority vote from at least two-thirds of the entire membership must be secured before the motion can be approved.

This is different from other motions wherein simply a majority vote would do for a motion to pass. If the votes for a motion does not reach the required number, then the motion will be defeated. An example of a situation wherein this would apply is when there is a motion to remove a member from the organization.

d. No member can demand for a higher vote than a majority vote on a particular motion. Exceptions to this rule can only be made possible if the bylaws of the organization or the parliamentary authority has specifically stated that a majority vote from two-thirds of the membership is required to settle a specific issue or topic.

e. Every member must be informed of the work being done by other members and officials in an organization. To prevent the spread of misinformation, reading the minutes of the previous meetings before an upcoming meeting is highly recommended.

The minutes would also be helpful for those who were absent during the previous meetings. Furthermore, members have the right to access the reports made by the board, committees, and other officials. If a member wishes to read or hear them, he or she may request a copy from the secretary of the organization.

For those who have just realized the many benefits of implementing the rules of order, it is important to maintain a high level of patience and endurance - particularly when just starting the process of adopting this in an organization. It may seem like it is too formal for your kind of organization, but over the years, people have managed to successfully apply its concepts and principles to all types and sizes of organizations.

If you believe that the rules of order could bring positive changes into how your organization is being run, then the extra effort and time that it will take for you to successfully master and implement them will be beneficial for everyone.

Chapter 4 – When and How You Can Use the Rules

The original objective of the manual, as envisioned by Gen. Robert, is to serve as a guide on parliamentary procedures for the members of a given group during meetings and decision-making. Fortunately, such an intention has been retained and even improved upon in the later editions of the manual.

The principles and procedures included in Robert's Rules of Order, therefore, shall apply to just about any kind of setting - be it personal, work, or organizational. Furthermore, Gen. Robert wanted everyone to apply parliamentary procedures in their daily lives, so he first wrote it in manner that would make the manual accessible and readable for anyone.

Given these points, it should not come as a surprise that Robert's Rules of Orders remains to be the most widely used governing document for all types of organizations, not just in the United States of America, but across all English-speaking countries in the world.

Even churches, with all of their centuries-old records and traditions, have come to rely on the principles and procedures of the manual in order to create and promote a harmonious congregation. Companies use Robert's Rules of Order in all their business meetings, from strategic planning sessions down to team briefing among staff members. The board of universities and non-profit organizations use the manual for similar purposes, which allows them to make quicker and more sound decisions as a governing body over their respective groups.

To further your understanding of the many applications of Robert's Rules of Order, here are the ways in which individuals and organizations implement the principles and procedures stated in the manual:

- ***Organizing and Facilitating Productive Meetings***

    Business meetings are conducted in order to provide the members a proper venue wherein they can participate in the creation and finalization of plans, decisions, and actions that will affect the organization.

    Applying the rules of order to meetings allows the members to organize meetings in an efficient manner. An agenda itemizing all items that must tackled during a meeting is one of the basic elements of the rules of order. By adopting this, organizations will be able to comply with the first principle of the parliamentary procedures, which promotes the idea of handling one piece of business at a time.

    Even though there's a prescribed method for how to implement the use of an agenda in business meetings, organizations are still given the freedom to modify this according to the requirements and preferences of the members. In most cases, the rules and guidelines given in the bylaws overrule the parliamentary authority. This means that if, for example, the organization wants to apply the rules of order, they may modify it according to how the members want the quorum of a particular meeting to be.

- ***Presenting and Debating Upon the Ideas or Proposals of the Members***

    When it comes to Robert's Rules of Order, the acceptable way of presenting an idea or proposal during a meeting is through the use of main motions. In order to maintain the proper order of business, a main motion must be made first by a member before it can be opened for discussion or debate within the assembly.

The rules of order specify how a motion can be brought forward to the attention of the chair and the other members, as well as how the members can initiate the discussion on this matter. There are also times when a member might behave in a manner that is disruptive or unhelpful to the discussion. In such cases, Robert's Rules of Order allows members to point out these negative actions and halt them immediately before they can cause further delay or damage to the organization.

Many people tend to ramble while talking about their ideas or opinions, especially when left unchecked. The rules of order have provisions that will allow members to impose a time limit on the discussion or debate, or even to question the point that the other member is trying to make.

It should be noted that Robert's Rules of Order promotes courtesy and civility among the members, so raising such points or making restrictive motions should always be done in a polite and respectful manner towards the chair and the entire membership.

- ***Using Votes as a Decision-Making Tool***

    Democracy is essential for a productive and effective organization. This can only be fully attained when every member has been given the right to vote. This means that each vote holds equal weight for every decision that has to be made, and that even those who have voted in the minority will still be heard by the rest of the membership.

    In a democratic organization, votes must also be taken in an objective and fair manner for everyone involved. Robert's Rules of Order addresses this requirement by giving specific rules on how to initiate, process, and tally the votes without violating the rights of members.

The majority rules in a democratic organization, but this does not mean that the minority are necessarily in the wrong. Even though the results of the vote have been announced, a member, especially if he or she is from the prevailing side, can still make a motion for the motion to be reconsidered by the other members. Those in the minority may then be given another chance to make their case, and potentially overturn the motion that has been adopted by the organization.

- **Electing Officers that are Capable and Qualified in Leading the Organization to the Right Direction**

    Robert's Rules of Order indicates that the organization's bylaws must include provisions that allow the members to nominate and elect officers that will lead the committees or the entire membership. In order to better implement this, the bylaws must be written in a detailed manner in order to specify the expectations of the members from their officers, as well as how long the officers are allowed to serve in their respective offices.

    A good bylaw shall also lay out the procedures as to how members can nominate individuals into each position, and how to remove elected officers in the case that there is a valid reason for such an action. These valid reasons must also be indicated in the bylaws in order to guide the members on this matter.

    Sometimes, officers may have to resign from their post for whatever reason. Therefore, the bylaws must have provisions for how to handle the resignation of officers, and how the members can assign or elect their replacements in order to ensure the continuity of the progress and business of the organization.

Again, parliamentary authorities, such as Robert's Rules of Order, serve as guides for organizations on how to best apply the rules and principles of the parliamentary procedures. If a particular rule or provision does not meet the requirements or preferences of the members, then the organization is free to create their own rules or modify the recommendations accordingly.

Robert's Rules of Order should not be used as a tool that will limit or restrict the ideas and actions of the members of the organization. Instead, it aims to provide a structure upon which an efficient and productive organization can be built.

Chapter 5 – Key Terms and Scripts to be Aware of

When it comes to stating a motion, Robert's Rules of Order specifies the correct terminology to be used in any kind of setting. By following the guidelines on this particular parliamentary procedure, the presiding officer will be able to repeat the motion to the rest of the group, thereby formalizing and acknowledging it.

Exact wording is important for making motions since this will ensure clarity among the members and in the documentation of the minutes of the meeting. Robert's Rules of Order explains that there are four main types of motion: main, subsidiary, incidental, and renewal. In special cases, the members may also make privileged motions. Each type of motion is assigned their corresponding terminologies that denote the intention and nature of the motion. Understanding the following keywords and phrases will allow you to learn how to properly use them during a meeting:

Main Motions

Among all types of motions, this is considered to be the most important one. A member can make a main motion in order to bring a particular subject to the attention of the assembly, and to call for an action to be made regarding the said subject. However, this can only be done when no other motion is being discussed or voted upon by the group.

A. **Key Terminologies for Main Motions**

- *Presiding Officer or Chair*

    This refers to the member that has been elected to lead and conduct the meetings of the organization. The formal title for the presiding officer is the "Chair", but this is not always used. In some cases, the members may refer to the presiding officer as the "president" instead.

- *Vote*

    When members wish to express their opinion, preference, or disagreement with a certain idea or proposal, they may do so formally by casting their votes. A vote can only be taken if there is motion that has already been put forward by a member of the group.

- *Ayes or Yeas*

    This pertains to an affirmative vote of a member of the group. Either of term may be used for voting.

- *Noes or Nays*

    When a member is against a given motion, he or she can vote by saying no or nay once called upon by the presiding officer during the voting part of the meeting.

- *Majority vote*

    If more than half of the members have voted for a certain side of the matter at hand, then it can be said that the said motion has gained the majority vote. The total count does not include, however, the number of absentees or abstention during that given meeting. For example, a majority vote can be declared if at least 31 out of 60 votes have been tallied for either side of the motion.

- *Two-thirds vote*

    If the votes on one side are at least twice as many compared to the other side, then that motion is said to have the two-thirds vote of the members. To illustrate this, a two-thirds vote can only occur when 10 members have voted aye, while only five members voted nay on a particular motion.

- *Adopted Motion*

    A motion that has been accepted by the members through voting is referred to as an adopted motion. This means that a majority of the members agree to the idea or action that has been proposed using the said motion.

- *Defeated Motion*

    When a motion fails to garner the majority vote, then it will be declared as defeated or lost. This means that not enough of the members agree with the contents of a given motion. Defeated motions, however, are not entirely dead since they may still be raised once more. A motion to reconsider the defeated motions can be made by a member and then approved by the assembly.

B. **Standard Script for Main Motions**

- Before putting forward your motion, you need to first obtain the floor. To do this you have to stand up and refer to the presiding officer in this manner:

  "Mr. Chairman/President" if the presiding officer is male or" "Madam Chairman/President" if the presiding officer is female.

- Once you have gotten their attention, you are now allowed to make the motion. You can do this by starting your statement, similar to the following examples:

  "I move to adjust the start of our lunch break from twelve noon to eleven thirty in the morning instead." or "I move that parking spaces for this building be reassigned according to tenure of employees."

- After taking your turn, the presiding officer will then repeat your motion to the assembly. The standard way of doing this is by seconding your motion and opening the floor for the assembly's reaction. To illustrate this, here is a sample statement:

  "The motion is moved and seconded that the start of the lunch break shall be adjusted from twelve noon to eleven thirty in the morning. Will there be any discussion about this?"

- To begin the voice voting process, the chair will state the following instructions for the assembly:

    "All in favor, say "yes." Those in opposition, say "no."

- After everyone has casted their respective votes by saying out loud their choice, the chair will announce which side has the majority, thereby determining the next action regarding the motion.

    If the majority is in agreement with the motion, the chair shall say:

    "The ayes have it by twenty votes. The motion is carried. We will be adjusting the start of the lunch break from twelve noon to eleven thirty in the morning. Mr. Smith from HR Department will implement this new policy."

    On the other hand, if the majority disagrees with the motion, the chair announces the defeat of the motion by saying:

    "The noes have it by twenty votes. The motion is lost. We will not be adjusting the start of the lunch break from twelve noon to eleven thirty in the morning."

- In the case of a rising vote, the chair gives the following instructions to the assembly instead:

"All those in favor of the motion, please rise from your seats."

After taking count of those who have stood up, the chair will then say:

"Be seated."

Next, the votes of those in disagreement will be taken:

"All those in opposition of the motion, please rise from your seats."

Again, after taking count of the negative votes, the chair will say to the assembly:

"Be seated."

- To announce the results of the rising votation process, the chair is going to state the following in the case the majority agrees with the motion:

    "The affirmative has it by ten votes. The motion is carried. We will be adjusting the start of the lunch break from twelve noon to eleven thirty in the morning. Mr. Smith from the HR Department shall implement this policy."

In the event that the majority disagrees with the motion, the chair announces this in the following manner:

"The negative has it by ten votes. The motion is lost. We will not be adjusting the start of the lunch break from twelve noon to eleven thirty in the morning."

- When someone is in doubt about the results of the voice votation process, the said member is allowed to express their thoughts by saying the following:

"I call for a division" or simply "Division."

The chair is required to acknowledge this request, saying:

"A division has been called by Ms. Harper."

From there, a rising vote shall take place in order to validate the accuracy of the number of votes for each side. After following the same process as the ones stated above regarding a rising vote, the chair must announce once more which side has the most votes. Any requests for further validation will no longer be entertained after the second round of taking votes from the assembly.

Subsidiary Motions

This type of motion is used to change the direction of how a main motion is being handled by the assembly. Given this, a member must make a main motion first before any subsidiary motion may be put forward.

A. **Key Terminologies for Subsidiary Motions**

- *Previous question*

    If a member wishes to bring the assembly to an immediate vote, he or she can make a motion to call for the previous question. This will stop the ongoing discussion or debate among the members, if it has gained a majority vote from two-thirds of the assembly.

- *Close debate*

    Similar to the motion to call the previous question, a motion to close the debate can also be made in order to proceed to the voting part of the meeting. Again, this motion is not up to the decision of the debate moderator only. The two-thirds majority of the entire membership must approve the motion for this to be adopted.

- *Limit or extend debate*

    If the subject at hand must be decided upon immediately, a member can make a motion to establish a specific amount of time that may be spent on debating the topic. Once approved, the secretary or another appointed person must monitor and impose the time limit given for that particular debate. When the time has elapsed, the group will then be asked to cast their votes.

- *Refer to committee*

    When a motion has been referred to a committee, the task of reviewing the motion will be given to a specific group within the organization. The group will then present the results of their evaluation to the assembly so that every member can be informed before the voting on the motion takes place.

- *Amendment*

    Typically, a motion is being amended in order to make it more acceptable for the majority of the group. The points for amendment must be directly related to the objective of the main motion that it is pertaining to. The amendment cannot be worded in such a way that would make the original intention behind the main motion appear like it has been defeated.

    There can be two amendments on the floor simultaneously. The first one should pertain to the main motion, while the second one modifies the first amendment. However, it should be noted that only one amendment may be discussed at a time. When it comes to voting, the amendments should be voted upon in reverse order according to how they were made, meaning that the second amendment must go first during the voting portion of the meeting.

- *Tabling*

    Tabling a motion means that the discussion about this topic will be postponed to a later date. When this is put forward, the group will stop considering the motion without need for further debate.

- *Postpone to a definite time*

    The effect of this motion is similar to tabling, except that the group must set a definite date and time for the continuation of the discussion.

- *Postpone indefinitely*

   When a motion has been postponed indefinitely, that particular idea can be considered as defeated. The only way to overturn this is to secure the vote of two-thirds majority.

B. Standard Script for Subsidiary Motions

- When someone wants to kill a motion, the member must state this intention in the following manner:

   "I move for the motion to be postponed indefinitely."

   The keyword in that statement is "indefinitely", which when granted, will effectively stop all discussions to be had and decisions to be made regarding the topic or issue.

- The chair, however, cannot promote or hamper this motion on his or her own. The request to kill a motion must be decided upon by the assembly, triggering a vote among the involved members. Given this, the chair will have to say:

   "The request is moved and seconded to postpone the motion indefinitely. Will there be any discussion regarding this request?"

- The assembly can either take a voice vote or a rising vote. The terminologies to be used and process to be followed is the same with taking a normal vote.

- However, announcing the results of the vote must be stated in a different manner. In the case of the majority agreeing with the requestor to kill the motion, the chair declares the following:

  "The ayes have it with five votes. The motion to postpone indefinitely is carried. This means that the motion is killed for the entirety of this meeting, but only if no one who voted in the affirmative will move to reconsider the vote. Is there any further business related to this?"

  If the assembly did not agree with the requestor's intention, the chair shall then announce the following statement:

  "The noes have it by five votes. The motion is lost."

  The chair will then proceed to ask if the assembly wishes to move back to the main motion prior to the denied subsidiary motion. If the assembly says aye, the chair will lead the group back to the original point of the discussion. However, if any member of the assembly wants to reconsider the vote, a division will be called, and another vote shall ensue.

- Sometimes, a member of the assembly may want to put forward an amendment to the main motion that has already been discussed by the group. To initiate this, the member must say:

  "I move to amend the motion by striking out the specified time of lunch break."

  Another way of making an amendment is by adding a certain condition to the original motion. For example:

"I move to amend the motion by adding at the end the names of those who are going to be affected by the adjusted time for lunch break."

You can also combine the two forms of amendment by saying this instead:

"I move to amend the motion by striking out the specified time of lunch break, and instead inserting the names of those who are going to be affected by the adjusted time for lunch break."

- Likewise, the chair has various ways of responding to the requested amendment. First, the chair can state the following:

"It is moved and seconded to amend the motion by striking out the specified time of the lunch break. If amended, the motion would read as follows: The start of the lunch break is adjusted to eleven thirty in the morning. Is there any discussion on the proposed amendment?"

When a condition has been proposed to be added to the original motion, the chair will say this instead:

"It is moved and seconded to amend the motion by adding the names of the affected individuals. If amended, the motion would read as follows: The start of the lunch break is adjusted from twelve noon to eleven thirty in the morning for Ms. Anna Harper and Mr.

Kenneth Smith. Is there any discussion on the proposed amendment?"

Combining the two responses to the request for amendment, the chair can also say:

"It is moved and seconded to amend the motion by striking out the specified time of the lunch break, and also adding the names of the affected individuals. If amended, the motion would read as follows: The start of the lunch break is adjusted to eleven thirty in the morning for Ms. Anna Harper and Mr. Kenneth Smith. Is there any discussion on the proposed amendment?"

- A vote among the members must be taken to decide if the amendment will be applied or not to the original motion. To start, the chair announces the following to the assembly:

"The question is on the adoption of the amendment proposed on the start of the lunch break for Ms. Anna Harper and Mr. Kennedy Smith. All those in favor, say "Yes." Those in opposition, say "No."

If the majority of members have voted "yes", the chair will then say:

"The yeas have it, and the motion is amended to indicate that the start of the lunch break has been adjusted to eleven thirty in the morning for Ms. Anna Harper and Mr. Kenneth Smith. Is there any further discussion on this?"

If not, the chair will announce the defeat of the motion to amend by saying:

"The noes have it, and the motion has been lost. Is there any further discussion on this?"

Incidental Motions

This particular type of motion is used for maintaining the order of the assembly. For example, a member can make an incidental motion whenever a rule is being overlooked or violated during a meeting. Due to its nature, incidental motions take precedence over both main and subsidiary motions.

A. Key Terms for Incidental Motions

- *Point of order*

    A point of order can be made if a member believes that a rule is being broken or violated by the other members or officers of the organization. Since this is not a formal motion, it can be called even if the member has not been recognized by the assembly. However, a ruling is required from the moderator in order to determine if this must be considered immediately.

- *Point of information*

    When a member has information related to the topic being discussed, he or she can raise a point of information in order to get recognition from the presiding officer.

- *Appeal from the decision of the chair*

    Any decision made by the chair can be overruled by the rest of the assembly. This motion would require a second, and if it has been made, it can no longer be amended further. It cannot be subjected to a debate if the appeal has been caused by a suspected misuse of power by the chair. In addition, this cannot be debated when there is already a motion to close the said debate.

- *Parliamentary inquiry*

    When a member wants to clarify a point being made during the discussion, he or she does not need to make a motion to get a direct answer from the presiding officer or the assembly itself. Instead, a parliamentary inquiry may be made instead in order to ask what actions would be done in response to the motion.

- *Division of assembly*

    This motion is used to request a method of counting votes that can produce more easily measurable results compared to simple voice votes. Common alternative options include requiring the members to raise their hands or to stand up as the votes are being counted.

- *Request to withdraw a motion*

    This motion is used to take back a motion that has been made by another member. A prevalent misconception among the beginning practitioners of parliamentary procedures is that the maker of a motion can withdraw his or her own motion. On the contrary, this motion must be made by any member other than the original member. Given this, a majority vote is needed in order to let this motion pass.

- *Suspension of the rules*

    Rules may be suspended when matters have to be taken out of order. However, since this motion can be made by anyone, at any time, and for whatever reason, a majority vote from at least two-thirds of the entire membership is required. While the rules are suspended, no decision or voting can be made by the assembly. Discussions may still continue until a motion to restore the rules has been made and adopted.

- *Object to consideration of the question*

    If a motion is believed to be both non-essential and designed only to disrupt the ongoing discussion or debate, an objection may be raised by any member. This will warrant a ruling from the chair to determine whether the objection is valid. If the ruling indicates that it is valid, the assembly must vote on whether the motion will be adopted or not. Otherwise, the objection can be summarily dismissed by the chair upon evaluation of the given motion.

B. Standard Script for Incidental Motions

- In order to make a point of order, a member must address the presiding officer and say:

    "I rise to a point of order."

The chair will acknowledge the member by saying:

"Please state your point."

- If a member wants to clarify a point during a discussion, he or she will have to say:

"Mr./Madam Chairman, I rise to a parliamentary inquiry."

The chair will then respond in this manner:

"Please state your inquiry."

- To make an appeal against a ruling made by the chair, a member should say:

"I am appealing the decision of the chair."

If the motion has been seconded, and it has been deemed debatable by the assembly, the chair will have to acknowledge the appeal of the member through this statement:

"The ruling of the chair has been appealed. The chair ruled that the start of the lunch break is officially adjusted to eleven thirty in the morning. The question is, shall the decision of the chair be sustained, or shall it be repealed? Is there any discussion on this?"

The assembly will then debate on the matter. Once they are done, votes must be taken in order to arrive at the members' final decision regarding the motion.

If the ayes have the majority vote, the chair shall announce the vote in this manner:

"The ayes have it. The ruling of the chair is sustained."

If the motion to appeal has been defeated, the chair shall announce this by stating:

"The noes have it. The ruling of the chair shall not stand."

Renewal Motions

If the members have already decided to take an action on a motion, a member can still request for the discussion to be restarted or for the action to be cancelled using renewal motions.

A. Key Terms for Renewal Motions

- *Reconsider*

    A motion to reconsider is going to be made if the group wants to restart the discussion about a motion that has been defeated earlier during the same meeting. This can only be adopted if the majority of the board or council has approved the request to extend the duration of the meeting in order to continue the discussion about the said motion.

- *Take from the table*

    This motion can be made if a particular motion has been tabled earlier but no date or time has been set for when the motion will be open for discussion again. This motion will require a vote from the majority, but there is no need for a debate to occur first before the votes of the members can be taken.

- *Rescind*

    An action can be annulled at any point in time once a motion to rescind has been adopted by the group. There are two ways as to how this motion can be passed. If the presiding officer has given prior notice to the assembly that a motion to rescind may be considered later on for a given motion, then a simple majority vote from all those present would suffice for this purpose. However, if there is no prior notice, there must an approval from at least two-thirds of the entire membership.

B. Standard Script for Renewal Motions

- For a motion to be reconsidered, a member shall state:

    "I move to reconsider the vote on the motion about the adjusted beginning time of the lunch break. I have voted on the prevailing side."

    Once the original motion has been seconded, the chair will have to respond to the request:

    "It is moved and seconded to reconsider the vote on the motion about the adjusted beginning of the lunch break."

If the motion is deemed to be debatable, the chair will then ask the assembly:

"Is there any discussion on this?"

When the debate is over, the members will be called once again to vote on the original motion. The chair will announce which side has prevailed using the same script for the votes on a main motion.

- In order to rescind a motion that has already passed the majority vote, a member must make the following motion:

"I move to rescind the motion that has been adopted to adjust the beginning time of the lunch break."

Once the motion receives a second, the chair will then respond by saying:

"It is moved and seconded to rescind the motion that has been adopted to adjust the beginning of the lunch break. Is there any discussion regarding this?"

If no previous notice was given, a two-thirds vote will be required from the assembly in order for the motion to rescind to be carried out. The chair will announce the vote in this manner:

"Since there has been no previous notice given regarding the motion to rescind, this would require a two-third vote before being adopted. All in favor, say "Yes." Those in opposition, say "No."

In the event that previous notice has been given, the chair will say:

"Because previous notice has been given, this motion will require a majority vote from the present members. All those in favor, please rise."

After counting the members that have stood up, the chair will then say: "Be seated. All those in opposition, please rise."

Again, the votes will be counted. The members will be asked to take their seats after all votes have been taken.

To announce that the motion has prevailed, the chair will either say:

"There are two-thirds vote in the agreement with the motion. The motion to rescind has passed and the previous action to adjust the beginning of the lunch break is rescinded."

Or:

"The ayes have it. The motion is going to be carried. The previous action to adjust the beginning of the lunch break is rescinded."

In case the motion has been defeated, the chair will say either:

"There is less than two-thirds in agreement with the motion to rescind. The motion is lost. The previous action stands as it has already been adopted."

Or:

"The noes have it. The motion has been lost. The previous action is going to stand as originally adopted."

Privileged Motions

There are certain points during a meeting wherein a member can make a privileged motion on behalf of the entire assembly, or for some particular members only. Such motions are still subject to the approval of the members, however, before they can be acted upon.

A. Key Terms for Privileged Motions

- *Fix the time for next meeting*

  This motion can be made at any point during the current meeting, even when a motion to adjourn has already been made by a member of the group. The motion must be seconded, but a debate among the members is not necessary. If there are further changes to be made, then another member can make a motion to amend the original motion made regarding this matter.

- *Adjourn*

    A meeting can be stopped if a motion to adjourn the meeting has been made and thus gained the vote of the majority. There is no need to debate on this matter, as long as it has been seconded before voting. If no one wants to make the motion to adjourn, then the chair can ask the assembly if there is still any business left on their agenda. Receiving no response from the assembly means that the chair can declare that the meeting will be adjourned immediately.

- *Recess*

    If you want to stop the meeting but only temporarily, then you can make a motion for a recess instead. The originating member, however, must state the exact time that the meeting shall be called back into order. Again, the motion for a recess requires a second, and it cannot be amended once it has already been adopted.

- *Point of Privilege*

    This may be raised during the course of the meeting if the welfare of a group may be compromised or violated. Even if another member has taken the floor, a member can raise this point. As long as it has been proven to be justified, then there is no need for a second, a debate, or a vote for the point to be recognized by the presiding chair, and for it to be adopted by the entire assembly.

- *Call for the orders of the day*

    If a member believes that the group has diverged from the agenda of the meeting, he or she may call for the orders of the day. This can be made even in the midst of another member's turn to speak. Seconding the motion is not required, as well as debates and voting among the members, provided that the call has been deemed as valid by the presiding officer.

B. **Standard Script for Privileged Motions**

- To ask for a recess in the middle of a meeting, a member will say:

"I move that the meeting will have a recess for 15 minutes."

The chair acknowledges the motion by saying:

"It is moved to recess for 15 minutes. All those in agreement, say "Aye." Those who do not agree, say "No."

Upon tallying the votes, the chair will announce which side has prevailed by saying either:

"The ayes have it. The meeting stands in recess for the next 15 minutes."

The gavel must then be rapped once in order to signal the start of the recess.

Or:

"The noes have it. The group will not have a recess. Is there any further discussion on this?"

- If the member is feeling the need to raise a point of privilege, the member will have to say:

"Mr./Madam President, I rise to a point of privilege with regards to my concerns on the welfare of the assembly."

The chair will then respond in this manner:

"Please state your point."

The member who has raised the point will then specify his or her points of concern. It can be that the temperature in the venue has risen or lowered down to uncomfortable levels, or that the lighting of the room has become too dark for them to properly view the presentation. After making his or her point, the chair will then issue the ruling on the privileges of the members.

Chapter 6 – How to Introduce the Rules to an Organization

For the success of an organization, the members and officers must learn how to work in harmony with one another. This can only be achieved if the following factors are present:

First, there must be a common and deep understanding of the purpose and objectives of the organization. This should be the starting and ending point of every action and decision made by the organization. If only a select few know the goals of the organization, then their path to success will surely be an uphill battle.

Second, each member must understand and comply with the rules of the organization. This will ensure that every transaction among the members and other parties is standardized, resulting in outcomes that are consistent with the organization's expectations.

Third, the members must also know their rights as individual parts of the whole organization vis-à-vis the expectations of the organization from them. By promoting this level of understanding, the organization will be able to create a democratic atmosphere, which is more conducive to carrying out effective and efficient means of achieving their objectives.

Focusing on the second factor, the organization must determine the best way to introduce the rules of order to its members. This is not a simple task of announcing that they are going to follow a parliamentary process, effective on a certain date. It involves careful planning and deliberation among the members themselves.

Normally, the adoption of parliamentary procedures into an organization can take anywhere from several weeks, up to a year, depending on the size of the organization and the determination of the members. To guide you on how you could introduce the rules of order into your organization, here are the key points that you must cover:

- Choose a parliamentary authority that best fits the requirements of your organization. In the United States, Robert's Rules of Order is among the most widely followed manuals due to its comprehensiveness and level of detail. It should be noted that this shall only serve a guide and reference since you have not yet established the rules of your organization. This means that you are not obliged to follow every single recommendation of the parliamentary authority, especially if it would be counterintuitive to the productivity of the organization itself.

- Hire a parliamentarian as a consultant for your organization. A parliamentarian is an expert on everything there is to know about parliamentary procedures. By tapping into their core competencies, the organization may be able to cut down the time it will take them to create the necessary governing documents for the organization.

  Having a parliamentarian on board would likewise make the implementation of the rules more effective and efficient. He or she would be able to point out the inconsistencies between the current practice of the members and the rules of order. In the case that you cannot find a parliamentarian, you can opt to hire a legal expert instead, provided that they have a background and experience in handling the requirements of a parliamentarian authority.

- Invest in external training programs and orientations for key members of the organization. Select ones that have an aptitude for this subject so that they will be able to better absorb the concepts and principles of parliamentary procedures. These members will then be able to cascade the information to the other members, which could cut down the cost compared to having everyone undergo the trainings and orientations.

- Start introducing the rules by implementing them one by one. Do not be frustrated by the expected learning curve for the adoption of the parliamentary procedures. Instead, try to pace yourselves by gradually incorporating the rules into your current practices. This will permit the members to grow accustomed with the rules that you are going to impose on them. As a result, the possible resistance and hesitation among the members will be lessened considerably.

- Once you have finalized the governing documents, especially the bylaws, publish and reproduce the said documents in both softcopies and hard copies. Your objective is to ensure that every member will have a copy or will have access to the governing documents that your organization has. By doing this, no member could claim later on that he or she is ignorant of the rules of order.

- To further lessen the likelihood of your members resisting or resenting the introduction and implementation of the rules, you have to explain to them the benefits of the rules for each member and for the organization as a whole.

    This will give them the motivation and incentive to try and keep up with the changes that are happening within the organization. In general, these benefits are linked to the third defining factor of the success of an organization: democracy. In order for you to better explain this to the other members of the organization, here are the ways in which democracy can be beneficial to everyone involved:

- A democratic organization is not ruled by a select few, but rather the will of the majority—if not the entirety—of the membership. The decisions and actions of the organization undergo the review and approval of members before anything can be finalized and carried out.
- Every member has the right to put forward an idea, speak to the assembly, and cast a vote depending on his or her preference.
- The leaders of the organization are chosen by the members through the election process. After the term has ended, an officer returns to their previous post as a member of the organization. There is no hierarchy of power since any member may be considered for any given position.
- There are mechanisms in place to check and balance the actions and decisions of each member and officer of the organization. If there has been a proven abuse of power or authority, anyone can make a motion to amend or rescind that particular motion.
- Given that all members have been granted with equal rights, every member also shares the same amount of responsibilities as one another.
- Transparency is exhibited since every record or document is subject to the review of the members.
- Even though the majority rules, the rights of the minority and those who are absent remain protected.

Please note that the members are not required to memorize the rules of order in order to apply them into the practices of the organization. They must, however, gain some familiarity with the rules, and learn why each rule matters in terms of the success of the organization as a whole.

Purchasing a copy of Robert's Rules of Order is advisable even if you already have this handy guide, and especially when you have just recently introduced the members to the concept of parliamentary procedures. The copy can serve as reference material when the members need to clarify a rule, terminology, or process, even while in the middle of a meeting.

If you do not want to invest yet in the manual, then you can also refer to any of the various websites that feature condensed versions of the Rules of Order. There are even sites that contain the previous versions of the book, all of which are downloadable and free of charge. For quick inquiries or clarifications, there are numerous blogs that explain how a particular situation or motion should be handled in compliance with the parliamentary procedures.

Having only one or a few experts on parliamentary procedures does not guarantee the successful introduction and implementation of the rules of order within an organization. There must be concentrated effort on the part of the chair and officers to promote the understanding of the rules among the members. This may be done by circulating summaries or holding practice sessions for every member of the organization. As can be attested by almost every organization that has applied Robert's Rules of Order, the best way to practice these rules and principles is in a group setting.

Chapter 7 – Important Governing Documents

Without the existence of written records and documentations of the rules, every organization would become a slave to the whims of its members. Without the rules, those in the majority could influence and alter the rules according to how the rules would best benefit them in achieving their own personal goals.

Because of this, the parliamentary procedures have undergone significant revisions. The need to protect the rights of each individual member - whether the member belongs to the minority or is an absentee - is ever-present, hence the need to formalize and standardize the defensive mechanisms that should be put in place around them.

Robert's Rules of Order has achieved this feat by requiring the development and implementation of governing documents by all types of organizations that practice the parliamentary procedures. Among these documents, the most commonly established is the organizational bylaws or constitution. In the document, the members of the organization may find various information about the organization itself, such as how it first came into being, what are its goals and missions vis-à-vis its nature and the opportunities and threats it is facing, and the scope and limitations of the document's authority over the members of the organization.

Aside from this, the bylaws also specify how changes to the organization are going to be handled, thereby making the process of adopting changes more difficult compared to the process of making a motion to amend or rescind an already adopted motion. With such rigidity, the bylaws are not only protecting the rights of the minorities and the absentees, but they are also ensuring the continuity and stability of the organization. This does not mean, however, that the bylaws aim to restrict the progress or improvement of the organization.

They only seek to control and monitor the actions of members to prevent the occurrence of any untoward behaviors towards other members, or towards the organization itself.

To give you a better understanding of the different governing documents, as specified by the parliamentary procedures, here is an overview of each document with its corresponding purpose, powers, and limitations:

- ***The Corporate Charter***

    For an organization to be considered as a corporation, it must apply first for a corporate status to the state it belongs to, or directly to the federal government. Once granted, an organization must establish its corporate charter indicating the legal name of the new corporation, the official address, and the primary purpose of the organization.

    Why does an organization need to apply for incorporation? The state allows only organizations with a corporate status to do the following:

    - Hold properties in its name
    - Create and exact contracts with other parties that are legally binding
    - Sue other entities or individuals, and be sued back in return
    - Protect members from the personal liabilities they have incurred as a result of their performance of duties to the organization
    - Establish and use a corporate seal for the organization

- Ensure the continuity of the operations and legacy of the organization

To start the process of incorporation, it is highly advisable for the organization to hire a lawyer with expertise on the state laws pertaining to this matter. In order to avoid future legal complications, the information indicated in the corporate charter must be thoroughly reviewed so as to filter out unnecessary information from the document.

Aside from having basic information about the organization, the corporate charter may also include the types and frequency of meetings held by the members, the names of the directors on the board, as well as the duration of the terms of the organization's existence. The document may also declare whether the organization is for profit or non-profit. Again, it is best to consult with a lawyer which information about the organization should be disclosed in the corporate charter.

Once a trustworthy and credible lawyer has been selected, the members are responsible for providing all information that the lawyer might need to produce a draft of the corporate charter. This draft would then be subjected to the review of the members. If everyone agrees with the content, then the document will be approved as a final draft. If not, the members may suggest points for improvement that will serve as a guide to the revisions that must be made by the lawyer.

To signify that the final draft has been approved, all involved members must sign the document. After that, the signed document must be sent to the secretary of state for further processing. In some cases, the secretary of state may also require the submission of the organization's bylaws. If this is required from you, then the documents that you have submitted to the secretary of state will be processed and returned back to your organization. From thereon, these documents will be collectively referred to as the Articles of Incorporation, or the Articles of Association, or Certificate of Incorporation.

Once you have these documents on hand, the corporate charter becomes a legal document that has precedence over the other governing documents of the organization. This means that no other documents can adopt a rule or concept that will run against what is already stated in the corporate charter.

Once established, the corporate charter is not something that should be locked inside a vault for safekeeping. This document should be made available for all members in case they need to refer to it. Furthermore, the secretary must always include the contents of the corporate charter in other governing documents so that it may serve as that document's foundation. Any document that must be revised should also refer back to the corporate charter in order to verify the consistency of the items for revision, versus the original documents.

- ***The Constitution and Bylaws***

    The consolidation of the rules established by the members and officials of an organization is known as the constitution or the bylaws. This distinction is important since it clarifies that the bylaws are not merely the parliamentary rules that other organizations also follow. The constitution and bylaws are unique to each organization that has developed the said governing documents.

    Separating the constitution and the bylaws from one another is not necessary. Typically, either one of these documents can serve the same purpose well enough. Many organizations, however, choose to go for bylaws instead of constitutions due to the former's focus on the organization's defining characteristics, as well as its modes of operations, and the relationships of its members amongst one another and towards the assembly itself.

Both the constitution and the bylaws contain important information that cannot be easily changed without notifying every member of the organization first. All changes must also undergo the review of the members before they can be approved for implementation.

- ***Rules of Order***

    To achieve an objective and efficient organization, it is important for the members to adopt a parliamentary authority that must be followed by everyone. Robert's Rules of Order is just one of the many manuals that are available nowadays to serve such a purpose. However, there may be certain sections of these documents that do not apply to the organization in question. The members might also want to do things differently as compared to how the parliamentary authority describes it should be done. For this reason, some organizations opt to create their own rules of order.

    Like the already existing types of parliamentary authority, an organization's rules of order specify how the members should transact with other members and officers, as well as what the roles and responsibilities of each member and officer are during meetings and general assembly.

    There is no standard process for developing your own rules of order. This will depend on the requirements of your organization, as well as the preferences of the members. For example, your organization might want to add more ceremonies to the start of meetings. The members may also require different orders of business for each type of meeting that is going to be conducted within a given period of time. Many organizations also have unique rules when it comes to nominations, voting, and elections.

It should be noted that organizations do not need to modify every single aspect of the parliamentary authority in order to create their own rules of order. These documents exist and are being followed for good reason. If you believe that the prescribed methods would suitably meet your requirements while also meeting the expectations of the members, then it would be best to simply adopt what is already stated in the parliamentary procedures.

Another important thing to keep in mind is that the rules of order must take into account the rights of all members, especially those who belong to the minority group. The authors of the parliamentary authority have considered this factor during the conception of their works, so you must also remember to consider how your modifications will affect every member of your organization.

A common mistake among beginners is the incorporation of the rules of order into the bylaws. The two documents should always be treated separately since each one covers different aspects of the organization. Both documents, however, may be included into one booklet that can serve as a comprehensive piece of reference material for members and officers alike.

Any changes in the rules of order, once established and adopted by the organization, must undergo the review and approval of the members before the document can be amended accordingly. Since this will cause a major shift in the organization, an amendment would require a majority vote from at least two-thirds of the membership.

- **Standing Rules**

    To help establish the proper administration of an organization, the members may also develop their own standing rules for meetings and assemblies. In order to initiate such a thing, a main motion must be made by a member, and if approved, the standing rules will remain in effect until another motion has been made to amend or rescind every rule or parts of it.

    Since the standing rules have only been established with the use of a main motion, a simple majority vote can be used to signify that the group is willing to adopt them. Similarly, a majority vote among the members can cause the rules to be suspended or rescinded, with or without prior notice to everyone in the organization.

    If the main motion for the standing rules is to last for a certain duration, the secretary must record them into a book called the "Standing Rules." When documenting these rules, it is important to take note of the final version of the rules as they have been formally adopted, as well as the starting date on which the rules would take effect.

    When the standing rules are rescinded by the members later on, the secretary will have to put a strikethrough over the rescinded rules. Beside this, would be the exact date of when the rule has been formally rescinded. This means that no standing rules will be deleted entirely from the book. By doing so, future members will be able to refer to the book for guidance on how they should administrate the organization.

    If you do not know where to begin in terms of documenting your organization's standing rules, then you may start with the practices that the members do without a clearly stated instruction from any officer or governing document. They simply do it since it has always been done in a certain manner by other members.

The parliamentary procedures refer to these actions as the organization's customs.

These practices are not entirely baseless in most cases. In general, customs are formerly motions on standing rules that have been adopted by previous members, and have since then been forgotten by the current members. This means that there may or may not be a written document indicating how a certain custom has come into being in the first place.

In the case that you wanted to look for these documents, some organizations tend to refer to these in a different way. The most common alternative names for the standing rules are "policy statements" and "guidelines."

Now that you have an overview of the important governing documents that an organization must have, you need to deepen your knowledge on the most vital one among them: the bylaws. Without this document, your organization will lose its structure, and there will be chaos among officers and members.

Bylaws are used to specify the rights that each member has as part of an organization. Given those rights, it is necessary to define as well the levels of authority and power that the whole membership has in terms of making decisions on behalf of the organization as a whole. With these definitions, everyone will know the scope and limitations of the privileges and responsibilities given to the board and the officers of the organization.

The bylaws are also used to determine the nature of the organization. It is said that an organization is democratic when the power is given to the assembly as a whole. The votes and opinions of each member and officer hold the same weight and value. On the other hand, when importance and power is bestowed upon the board and the officers only, then the organization is considered to be authoritarian.

The individuals responsible for developing and establishing the bylaws must take great care in evaluating which of these formats will best fit the visions and missions of the organization. Some groups believe that it is better to leave decision making to those in charge, typically the board of directors. The majority of organizations, however, believe that there must be a balance between the powers given to the officers and of the whole assembly to keep things operating smoothly and objectively.

Composition

When the need to define the structure of an organization arises, it is best to follow the prescribed format for creating bylaws. Described below are the important topics that must be covered in the document. However, it should be noted that this is not set in stone. You should always keep in mind the requirements of your organization and adjust the contents of your bylaws accordingly.

Following the basic format of the bylaws, on the other hand, will save you time in the development phase of this document. If not, you will have to arrange for a series of extended meetings among the members so that you can discuss, debate, and vote upon the information that should be included or excluded from the bylaws. This is within the requirements of the parliamentary procedures, but for the sake of efficiency, it is better to draft first a preliminary version following the basic format, and then arrange for a meeting so that the draft can be reviewed in its entirety by the members.

To make the process even easier, you have to start by defining first the main purpose of your organization. Why does it exist? How does its existence help its members, or society as a whole? Next, you have to decide who will bear the power to make decisions for the organization. When you have answered these questions, then you will be able to complete the rest of the bylaws with greater ease and a more defined direction.

- *Article No. 1: The Name of the Organization*

    The bylaws will only state the name of the organization if it has not been formally incorporated yet, or if no organizational constitution has been established at the time of its development. This will prevent any conflict with regard to the proper and legal name of the organization.

    There have been many cases where the name of the organization is not consistently written across different governing documents. This typically occurs when the bylaws are produced first before the corporate charter. Since the latter is a legal document, the name of the organization cannot be exactly the same as another organization. In such instances, the one who has applied first for a corporate charter will have the right to bear the name.

    To avoid this mistake, it is perfectly fine to leave out this article in the meantime, especially if you have not yet formalized the name of your organization. You can simply refer to it in general terms such as the "company"

    or the "organization."

- *Article No. 2: The Purpose of the Organization*

    In this section, you will have to define the objectives of your organization. It is best to keep the statements brief and straight to the point. The main questions that you have to answer at this point are the following:

    - Why does your organization exist?
    - What is your organization supposed to do and achieve?

If you choose to use long answers to these questions, then you may opt to break them down using semi-colons between each significant point. This will make it easier and quicker for the readers to comprehend your answers.

The purpose of your organization also sets the limitations for what your members have to do in order to contribute to the stated goals of the organization. If a certain member wishes to expand his or her roles and responsibilities, but the current purpose of the organization does not support this motion, then a vote must be taken before this section could be amended in order to accommodate the corresponding shift in the nature of the organization.

- ***Article No. 3: The Members of the Organization***

    This particular article is broken down into multiple sections in order to define the types of members that the organization has, as well as the expected dues and the responsibilities assigned to each member.

    o *Section No. 1: Types of Members*

    For this section, you must determine if your organization will break down its membership into different classes. The typical classifications used by organizations are active, inactive, and honorary members. You may want to further define these categories according to the nature and requirements of your organization.

    The definitions of each type must highlight how one class differs from the others. If there are differences in terms of the members' rights during meetings, then you must explain this in the definitions as well.

The bylaws should also include information on how a member can become part of a specific class. In some cases, organizations likewise indicate if there are any limitations to the number of individuals for each type of membership.

- *Section No. 2: Eligibility of Members*

    The contents of this section determine how an individual can become a member of the organization. Are you going to require them to undergo written tests or interviews? Will you require a certain degree of expertise in a particular skill or area of interest? Will you impose restrictions based on the gender, age, or educational attainment of the person? Some organizations also filter out their membership based on geographic locations.

    Organizations that are open to the public must be extra careful in this section, however. Otherwise, their selection process might appear discriminatory against certain types of people. This can then cause some irreparable damage to the reputation and image of the organization.

- *Section No. 3: Dues or Fees to be Collected from the Members*

    In this section, you must specify the types and schedules of dues that will be imposed on the members, as well as the exact amounts that will be collected from each member. For example, let's imagine that your organization requires a $50 annual membership fee, which is collectible during the first month of a given year. Any changes to the amount or schedule of the fee may only be carried out if its corresponding section in the bylaw has been amended first.

There are some organizational bylaws that indicate that the board may establish the dues for the entire membership on a yearly basis. If this is the case for your organization, then you must also specify in the bylaws the allowable percentage of increase per year in order to keep things fair among the members and the organization itself. Another way of handling this is by announcing first the proposed increase, and then having it reviewed and ratified by the members of the organization.

In case there is a different fee for each type of membership, the bylaws must break down the structure of the dues accordingly as well. Everyone should be made aware of the collectible dues from each member, even if that individual does not belong in a particular group. This will show that the organization is being transparent and objective among its members.

Aside from the amount and schedule of payments, it is also important for the bylaws to explain when a member will be considered as a delinquent because of unpaid dues. Following this, the bylaws must then indicate the fines or penalties that the member will incur due to his or her failure to pay completely and on time. It should be noted that no one in the organization can prohibit a non-paying member from attending meetings and other group functions, unless it is stated otherwise in the bylaws.

Protections for the members must also be set in place in the bylaws. Information about the payment procedures, including the name of the appointed person who is authorized to receive and process the payments of the members, should be clearly stated in the document.

The amounts and schedules of dues must also be emphasized well enough so that no one can take advantage of any member by charging them more than what is actually expected from them. For example, if the membership fee is a one-time payment, the bylaws must indicate this in clear terms so that the member will not be charged on an annual basis instead.

- *Section No. 4: Membership Requirements*

The organization should specify its expectations from its current members. Many require their members to attend a certain number of meetings per year. Failing to do so might result in a penalty for the member, suspension of membership, or in the case of recurring failures, complete revocation of membership.

Depending on the nature of the organization, the members may also be required to fulfill certain duties or conduct activities outside of their current responsibilities within the organization. For example, members might be required to attend trainings and seminars held by other organizations in order to further their knowledge or skills. Others might require their members to take part in the different committees established within the organization. Such requirements should include the rationale behind them so that the members do not question the intentions of the organization.

- *Section No. 5: Disciplinary Actions and Procedures*

    Some organizations choose not to include this one, but it can be quite beneficial, especially for new organizations who are unfamiliar with the parliamentary procedures. When writing this section, extra care must be exercised in identifying the behaviors that would warrant a disciplinary action. Consequently, it is also important to be careful when assigning the corresponding disciplinary actions. Consistency and reasonableness are two key factors that must be considered during this step of the development process.

    In the case that you do not want to expend too much effort on this aspect of your organization, you may simply refer to the existing parliamentary authorities available to you. Typically, a section on disciplinary actions is included in these manuals. Once you have ascertained that your chosen parliamentary authority contains information on this, you may rely on it when it comes to enacting disciplinary measures among the members of the organization.

- *Section No. 6: Resignation of Members*

    Organizations must set a provision for members who wish to revoke their membership. This should specify the steps that the member must take to withdraw their membership, as well as any consequences or fees that the process will entail. There must also be a system in place for those individuals who want to return to the organization.

- ***Article No. 4: The Officers of the Organization***

    In this article, all information relevant to the officers of the organization must be documented and laid out in clear terms. There must be a list of responsibilities assigned for each office, as well as the privileges granted to each one of them. The process of nominating and electing officers must be specified to guide the members in conducting these processes in the future. Please take note that the officers must be listed down according to their rank, and that all directors must be classified as officers of the organization as well.

    - *Section No. 1: Position Titles of Officers*

        In the very beginning of this section, you must declare outright the positions of the officers according to their rank. For instance, you could write down the following opening statement: "The officers of this company are the chairman, the chief executive officer, chief operating officer, chief financial officer, corporate secretary, and five directors."

        Following this, you need to indicate that all of these officers are expected to serve their offices and perform their duties according to the contents of the bylaws and the parliamentary authority. If you wish to list down each of their duties and responsibilities, brief and direct statements are highly recommended for this section of the bylaws. If there are too many duties, you may opt to write a separate article for these instead.

        The authors of the bylaws must be careful when listing down the duties and responsibilities of each officer. Any omission might send a message that there is no such requirement that is expected from that particular officer. Similarly, if the author has committed a mistake in this section, the officers might encounter future conflicts and misunderstanding among themselves.

Minimizing the likelihood of the latter scenario may be achieved through the thorough review of this article. On the other hand, preventing the occurrence of the first unfortunate situation can simply be done by including the following phrase into the list of each officer's duties and responsibilities: "Handle other tasks given or made appropriate as stated in the organization's chosen parliamentary authority, or through the adoption of motions."

- Section No. 2: Procedures for Nominations and Elections

    Information about the nomination and election procedures must be detailed in this particular section. If the organization chooses to delegate the responsibility of nominating officers only to a certain group of members, then the bylaws must state who in the organization will select the members who will join the nominating committee.

    This particular committee is the only committee that the current president may not be a part of - not even during the selection process. The best way to designate a nominating committee is through an election among the members of the organization.

    The duties and responsibilities as well as the limitations of the nominating committee must also be included in the bylaws. Are they allowed to nominate only one candidate per office, or can they nominate multiple individuals for each position? If you have not yet written this part of the bylaws, then you must specify the allowable number of nominations for each office.

This section likewise covers the process and schedule of the elections. Included in here as well is the prescribed method of voting among the members. In general, most organizations choose to vote through the use of a ballot in order to keep their choices private and objective. This particular method, however, is normally done when there is more than one nomination for the vacant position.

In case that there is only one nomination, organizations tend to do a voice vote instead. Other means of voting are acceptable, including sending votes through the mail, through email, or other electronic means of communication.

In addition, the bylaws should specify what the members will do to determine the winner of the election if they require something more than just the majority vote. In case of a tie, a procedure must be established to serve as a reference point for members in the future.

- *Section No. 3: Eligibility of Officers*

    The bylaws should state in clear terms how a member can become eligible to be nominated and elected into a particular office. You may either choose to explain this in general terms for all offices, or in specific terms for each position.

- *Section No. 4: Terms of Office*

    The organization must state in the bylaws when a particular term should begin and when it should end. The term limitations must be stated clearly so that there will be no confusion among the members when the time for another election approaches.

    If the beginning of the term is not specified in the bylaws, the officers will have to assume their office at the time of the election. For example, if a member has been elected as the new president, he or she will have to immediately take over the meeting in place of the former president. Rather than forcing a member to do something that they are not prepared for—which may also cause disruption in the meeting—it is best to establish a later date, after the meeting has ended, as the official start of the officer's term in the office.

    There can also be another point of confusion between the incumbent officer and the newly elected officer. If it is not clarified in the bylaws, the office might end up having no officer to serve the duties expected from them. To avoid this, the bylaws should state when the official transfer of duties will commence between the two officers.

    In case that the current term has ended but there is still no new elected officer to take over, the incumbent officer will have to remain in office and continue to perform his or her duties until the members have elected a replacement.

    Electing different members after each given term is healthy for the organization. In order to ensure this rotation of officers, the bylaws must state the allowable number of consecutive terms for each position.

- Section No. 5: Removal from the Office

    A provision for the removal of an officer from his or her current position must be included in the bylaws. In this section, the organization may state that the removal must have a just cause, or if they will be able to remove any officer without cause. In the case of the former, the list of probable causes has to be declared for everyone's knowledge. For the latter, a majority vote from two-thirds of the membership must be secured in order for this removal to become effective.

- Section No. 6: Office Vacancies

    Though similar to the act of removing an officer from his or her position, including a separate section for office vacancies is necessary when it comes to developing the bylaws of your organization.

    Aside from giving specific directions for how to fill a vacancy in an office, this section contains information on how to declare a vacancy in case the officer failed to attend the required number of meetings for that specific position. A member who wishes to declare a vacancy should undergo the process of making a motion, and then securing a two-third majority vote before their declaration can be considered as valid.

- **Article No. 5: Types of Meetings of the Organization**

  This article contains important information about the schedule of meetings, as well as the quorum and types of business that must be discussed by the members during the meeting. Provisions for special meetings are also specified so that the members will know when such activities may be conducted.

  o *Section No. 1: Schedule of Meetings*

    This section must begin with a declaration of the exact days on which the meetings will be held by the organization. For example, if you have a regular general assembly meeting every month, you may state this in the bylaw in this manner: "Every second Monday of every month, a general assembly will be conducted." You do not have to state the exact time and duration of the meeting since the standing rules contain this information already.

    Even meetings conducted on an annual basis must be stated clearly in this section. For instance, you might use this statement in your bylaws: "The annual meeting of shareholders is going to be held on the first week of June."

    Aside from the schedule, the types of businesses that may be discussed or transacted upon by the members during each meeting should be specified in the form guidelines. To illustrate this, you may want to add this guideline to your general assembly meeting: "During a general assembly meeting, the members may present and listen to the reports of officers and committees, as well as nominate, vote, and elect new officers into vacant positions."

Stated in this section are the forms of notifications that must be sent out to the members whenever a meeting is going to be conducted. The preferred method of notification—such as via mail, email, fax, or phone call—as well the timing of the notifications has to be clearly defined so that the secretary will be guided accordingly, and the members know what to expect in terms of the meeting notifications of your organization.

- *Section No. 2: The Quorum*

    The quorum refers to the required minimum number of attendees for any given meeting. This should be established in the bylaws of your organization so that you will be able to determine if the meeting or election shall go ahead.

    In establishing the quorum of a specific meeting, you must declare the exact number of attendees, instead of merely a percentage of the entire membership. For example, if the total number of members in your organization is 100, but only 40 members normally attend the meetings, then you should set the quorum at 40 members only.

    There is no standard number that is acceptable for a quorum to be established. Therefore, the organization does not need to set a high number that is out of the realm of possibility among the current members. Otherwise, the organization will run the risk of having no accomplishments whatsoever in terms of meetings and elections.

- Section No. 3: Special Meetings

    Special meetings may be called in the case that there is an emergency that the members need to attend to immediately. However, officers and members can only do this if the bylaws have a provision for special meetings in the first place. Without this, a special meeting might become a chaotic affair that could lead to further complications for the organization.

    In this section of the bylaws, you must indicate who exactly among the members are allowed to call a special meeting. This may be limited to the officers only, or you might also want to specify a select group of regular members as well.

    The procedures for calling and conducting a special meeting must likewise be specified in this section. In case certain members are allowed to do so, how many signatures in the petition must they collect before their request could be considered as valid? If the officers are the only ones allowed to call special meetings, how do they arrange it and notify the rest of the members? Do the notifications need to be sent out in advance, or would the members accept last-minute meeting invitations? These are some of the important questions that must be addressed in this particular section of the bylaws.

    To further save on time—especially since special meetings are urgent by nature—the bylaws may impose a restriction among the members that only business related to the original topic for discussion may be brought up during special meetings. Regardless of whether or not this is stated, it is common knowledge that unrelated business may not be added to the agenda without due process. However, since special meetings are unlike regular meetings, a separate provision for this reminder is necessary for all members of the organization.

- Section No. 4: Cancellation of Meetings with a Regular Schedule

   There are various reasons for a meeting to be cancelled. Under the parliamentary procedure, personal activities or emergencies are not considered valid reasons, but those that fall under the categories of force majeure or national-level emergencies would be more than enough reason to cancel a meeting.

   When the organization's bylaw includes a provision for this, it should be stated there who among the officers is responsible for deciding if a meeting will continue, or if it will be cancelled instead. Procedures on how to notify the rest of the members must also be established, as well as the process for how to reschedule the meeting to a later date.

- Section No. 5: Meetings through New Types of Media

   If the organization is willing to expand their means of communication to new forms of technology, then the bylaws must indicate how the members are going to utilize this in terms of conducting and attending meetings. There is a wide array of options that may be considered in lieu of face-to-face meetings. Many organizations now allow meetings through the use of webcams so that even those who cannot be present physically can still take part in the discussion.

In the event that their votes are needed, some organizations allow their members to send in their votes through email instead of the traditional means of writing their votes down on ballots.

Other than the bylaws, the provisions for these types of meetings must be covered in the standing rules. In that document, there should be a detailed account for how to arrange and facilitate meetings using the chosen new forms of media.

- *Article No. 6: The Executive Board*

This article allows the creation of a board for the organization. If this has not been included in the bylaws, then the elected officers may not act as if they are part of a board.

The coverage of this article includes the identification of the board members, how they can be elected to the board, and the total number of board members to be in the whole organization. Explained in this article are the duties and responsibilities of the board members towards the organization and the rest of the members, as well as other important information on how they should conduct their business during meetings and other parliamentary activities.

During the course of the development of this article, it is important to keep in mind that members cannot simply revoke any duties and responsibilities that have already been given to the board. Only when the specific duty is not formalized in the bylaws can the said duty be revoked by the members by making and voting upon a motion to rescind it.

For example, let's assume that according to the agreed upon bylaws, one of the duties of the board is to buy and sell properties in the name of the organization. The members cannot make a formal complaint to the assembly if the board decides to buy a property without consulting the other members of the organization first. The bylaws have given them the power to do so, and since the members have all agreed on this, it shall remain effective unless it has been officially amended.

To ensure that the democratic nature of your organization will be protected from the personal interests of the few, it is important to be specific in the bylaws about who has the power to do something on behalf of the entire membership. If your organization decides that all members should meet on a quarterly basis, then the board would not typically have great powers over the direction and decisions of the organization as a whole.

- *Section No. 1: Composition of the Executive Board*

    In this section, you should indicate the maximum number of members for the board of your organization. You must also explain how an individual can become part of the board. Is this exclusive only to the elected officers from various offices of the organization? Or are regular members allowed to be voted onto the board?

    Sometimes, organizations allow officers to join the board by virtue of them holding other offices within or outside the organization itself. For example, the mayor of the town where a school is located may have been elected to the board by the simple virtue of the mayoral office that he is currently serving in.

- Section No. 2: Meetings of the Executive Board

    The board must meet regularly in order to discuss important matters, transact business with one another, and make decisions that will impact the entire organization. Because of this, it is important to establish the structure and frequency of board meetings in the bylaws.

    Important information that must be included in this section are the types of meetings that the board must conduct, the quorum for each meeting, and the nomination, voting, and election requirements in case that a simple majority vote will not suffice.

    You must also determine whether or not the board may call special meetings among themselves. If that is going to be allowed, then you have to define which of them will be assigned to arranging for and facilitating the special meetings. Adding provisions for the cancellation, postponement, and rescheduling of board meetings would also be helpful for your organization.

    In the case that your organization has a small board, it is advisable to insist upon the majority vote to be from the entire board, instead of just merely those who have attended the board meeting. For example, let's assume that your board has six members in it. During one meeting, a vote has been taken, but only three members are present. If only a majority vote would suffice, then two out three votes would mean that the motion will be adopted. However, if you have specified that there should be a majority vote from the entire board, then the two ayes would not be enough for the motion to be carried forward.

Following the given example above, if you have set a quorum of three members for the board meeting, then all three of the attendees must be in agreement in order for the motion to be adopted. Anything less than that would not be considered as a win for the motion.

- *Section No. 3: Removal from the Board and Vacancies*

    This section of the bylaws addresses the various issues that may arise when it comes to the removal of certain members of the board. Some of the common issues faced by organizations on this matter are as follows:

    - Is the board allowed to remove one of their members on their own, or does the entire membership need to be consulted first regarding this?
    - If one of the members is a habitual absentee for multiple and consecutive board meetings, can the members of the board declare a vacancy and open up the position to other eligible candidates?
    - In the event that one of the members has resigned, can the board choose who the replacement will be, or will this trigger an election wherein the members can participate in the nomination and selection process?

- *Section No. 4: Duties of the Board Members*

    For this section, take the time to enumerate the duties and responsibilities of the board members.

Typically, these items are applicable to all members, but in some cases, special duties are assigned to key members of the board—the chair of the board, for instance. If the board has been granted the power to create committees and appoint members to each one of them, then you should also include that information in this section.

To better guide you in setting up this article, here are some points for consideration that you should keep in mind while writing the provisions:

    a. Is the board allowed to make their own rules as long as those rules do not run against the established rules of the organization?

    b. Can board members still be part of their respective committees as ex members?

    c. What is the extent of the powers bestowed upon the board members? Are they allowed to spend the funds of the organization by entering contracts with other entities, and purchasing assets? Are they allowed to sell or lease the properties owned by the organization?

    d. Does the board serve as the organization's official representative when it comes to transactions with government agencies and the general public?

    e. Are the board members allowed to hire or terminate the employees of the organization?

    f. Will the organization provide separate monetary compensation for the members of the board?

- *Article No. 7: Types of Committees Within the Organization*

    All standing committees within an organization must be recognized in the bylaws for them to be considered as valid and active. Common examples of such sub-groups include social, auditing, membership, program, and finance committees. In this article, the authors must define the total number of members for each committee, and then define each member's respective duties and responsibilities towards the achievement of their committee's objectives.

    The bylaws can also specify how long each member can serve for a given committee, thereby assuring the steady rotation of members assigned to each position. In the case that there is no need for an election, the bylaws may set out provisions for ad hoc committees, wherein the members are assigned to their posts by the board themselves.

    In terms of vacancies, the bylaws must state how the members would go about having these positions filled out properly. Resignations of committee members must also be defined so that everyone knows to whom the resignation should be addressed.

    Typically, committees are given their own budgets, or if not, are allowed to raise their own funds. Because of this, it is important to indicate in the bylaws as well if the committee is allowed to freely spend their funds, or if an authority figure has to be assigned to monitor and approve their income and expenditures.

- *Article No. 8: The Parliamentary Authority*

    In this particular article, the members must agree on which type of parliamentary authority will be adopted by the organization. It should also specify which edition of the manual will serve as reference for the members. For example, Robert's Rules of Order is one of the most widely used parliamentary authority across all types of organizations in English-speaking nations around the world.

- *Article No. 9: Amendments to the Bylaws*

    This article contains information as to how amendments to the bylaws should be initiated, discussed, voted, and adopted by the members of the organization. Since this will definitely entail major changes within the assembly, it is important to notify all members upon receiving the proposal. Only proposals that have received the two-thirds majority vote may be adopted as an amendment to the bylaws. Please take note that this article does not contain the exact amendments made to the bylaws. Those articles should be attached as an addendum to the current bylaws to reflect the changes made to the original version of this governing document.

Aside from the given articles of the bylaws, the organization is free to add content to the document as long as it meets the requirements of its members. These nine articles just form the the basic outline that can apply to every type of organization there is.

There are also certain clauses that could apply to organizations with specific purposes or needs. For example, if you are running a non-profit organization, then it would be best for you to include an indemnity clause into your bylaws. This means that your organization shall be legally exempted from any liabilities, charges, or penalties that may be brought about by the actions of any official member of your organization. Some states do require this clause for non-profit organizations, so it is advisable to consult legal experts on these matters.

Another important clause that you might want to add into your own bylaws is the dissolution clause. When this has been set in place, you will be able to pre-determine what will happen to the assets, funds, and properties of the organization in the case that it would be dissolved in the future.

If you find yourself having a hard time creating the bylaws for your organization, then attorneys and parliamentarians can lend you a helping hand in drafting this document. However, if you wish to push through with this endeavor, then you should keep in mind the following tips for writing bylaws:

- Use words that are easy to understand, and are direct and to the point.

- Avoid using legal terms or words that denote similar meanings in a single sentence. For example, "ratify" and "confirm." Even though both indicate approval, they denote the sentiment in varying degrees, which could later on confuse the end-users.

- State your sentences in a direct manner so that the reader will not have to refer to previous or succeeding sentences in order to make sense of what you are trying to say.

- If applicable, indicate the exceptions or qualifications to the terms or conditions that you are setting out.

If your organization is just starting out, the bylaws should only include what is currently in place, not what the organization is trying to be. It should be simple and usable for all members and officers.

As the organization continues to expand, the transactions within the organization will likely become more complicated, which could then lead to conflicts and problems between the members. At this point, you may consider revising and amending the bylaws so that they can adapt to the new requirements of your organization.

It is nigh impossible to predict the organization's trajectory of growth and the various problems that may arise. Therefore, it is advisable for the members to continue reviewing the bylaws on a regular basis, and check if there are any points for improvement to be made. This responsibility also serves as an opportunity for the members to ensure that their rights are still being protected, and that their organization is functioning at its best.

Chapter 8 – Using Minutes in Your Meetings

One of the primary responsibilities of the secretary centers on keeping the minutes of the meeting. This is a basic parliamentary record that all organizations must have in order to ensure the efficient and effective continuity of their operations. Since every organization has their own version of what should be included in the minutes, there seems to be a prevalent confusion, especially among beginners, on what should be included and what should be left out.

The answer is pretty simple. To figure out what the important contents of the minutes really are, refer back to the parliamentary authority that you have chosen to adopt for your organization. Guidelines and recommendations are given there by experts, typically with a thorough explanation as to why the inclusion of such information would matter in the long run.

You do not have any obligation to completely follow the parliamentary authority, however. The best way to go about this is to compare the written recommendations of the manual versus the wishes and requirements of the members of the organization itself. This should help you to come up with a format that will work best for the objectives of your organization while still remaining compliant with the parliamentary procedures.

Contents of the Minutes

The minutes are not merely a transcript of what has been said during the meeting. Rather, it is a tool to document what has happened during the entirety of the meeting. Following this concept, any personal opinions or interjections from the participants of the meetings should not be included in the official record.

The minutes should also bear a mark of approval from the assembly, signifying that the contents are true and valid. Once the minutes have been approved, it will then be considered as the final version of that particular record.

Oftentimes, the secretary (together with the presiding officer of the meeting) will go over the draft of the minutes to verify its completeness and accuracy. They could also discuss the proper wording used in the minutes, but the presiding officer cannot force a particular wording if the intention behind it is to make him or her appear better, or to change the results of the votes taken during the meeting.

In the event that a mistake has been found after the minutes have already been approved, then the secretary can bring the points for correction to the attention of the other members of the organization. A member, or even the chair, will then have to make a motion so that the secretary can amend what has already been adopted. From there, a vote will be taken among the present members in order to secure their consent on the revisions that are to be made.

Well-written minutes allow the reader to visualize what has transpired during a given meeting. This can be achieved with the use of proper writing and editing techniques. Writing and finalizing the minutes immediately after the meeting has ended will also help improve the quality of the output. The details of the meeting are still in the forefront of your mind, thereby allowing you to focus entirely on your writing instead of recalling key information from the meeting.

If the minutes are going to be published within or outside of your organization, the record should indicate the list of the members who were present. If there are any committee reports presented during the meeting, these should also be included and printed in full so that the readers can peruse them as well.

Structure and Layout of the Minutes

The secretary's extent of knowledge on parliamentary procedures is key to the accurate documentation of the minutes of the meeting. He or she must know the rankings of motions, as well other important parliamentary procedures, so that such information is written down in accordance with the rules of order. Furthermore, a knowledgeable and experienced secretary can be a valuable asset for the presiding officer in case that the organization's parliamentarian is not present for a given meeting.

It can take several hours of training and reading for the secretary to master the parliamentary procedures, especially those that pertain to the minutes of the meeting. Fortunately, Robert's Rules of Order specifies the important information that must be included in each section of the minutes. To help you better understand what constitutes a well-written and comprehensive record, here is a rundown of how a secretary should go about in recording the minutes of the meeting:

A. *The Opening Paragraph*

The following items must be included at the beginning of every minutes:

- *Call to Order*
    - The official name of the organization
    - Actual date and time that the meeting has started
    - Venue of the meeting, if it not the standard meeting place
    - Type of meeting to be conducted—regular, adjourned, or special

- Names of the presiding officer and the secretary assigned to the meeting. If they are not present, indicate the names of their substitutes instead

- Roll call, but only if it is indicated as a requirement in the rules of order. Record which of the members are present and which are absent. Take note also if a member has arrived late for the meeting, or has left earlier than expected

- *Approval of Minutes Taken from Previous Meetings*

The secretary must indicate if the minutes have been approved, or if certain corrections have been made. In the event of corrections, the secretary must take note of both meetings; the first being the one wherein the mistake first occurred, and the other one where the minutes have been read.

To illustrate this, here is an example of how the minutes should reflect the corrections and what actions should be done to formally correct the minutes:

Your minutes indicate that there should still be a balance of $1,000 in the treasury fund. However, upon review, it was verified that only $500 remains in the fund. To read this correction during the meeting, the secretary may say: "The minutes of the meeting taken on 27 May have been corrected to read 'the balance in the fund is $500 only.' The minutes have since then been approved as corrected."

If no one objects to this, the secretary will revise the corresponding minutes by putting a strikethrough over the "$1,000" and write "$500" instead. Beside this, the secretary is required to affix his or her initials. Depending on the parliamentary authority being followed, the secretary may likewise be required to write down the exact date on which he or she initialed the correction.

B. *The Body of the Minutes*

In this section, the secretary must document the details of the meeting. The following items may or may not have headings for each, but for the sake of readability, assigning a header for each is recommended.

- *Reports and Presentation of Committees and Officers*

    The secretary shall take note of the fact that the officers, board members, or committees—either special or standing—have given their reports in front of the assembly. Any actions that must be taken after the report must also be documented.

    For parliamentary authority, the secretary is required to provide a brief summary of the given reports. Others only require for the treasurer's report to be included in its entirety, though organizations tend to document only the key information derived from that report, such as the beginning and ending balances, gross income, and total expenditures.

- *Election of Officers*

    This portion of the minutes is only applicable if an election has been conducted during the meeting itself. If this is the case, then the secretary is going to record which members have received nominations, the number of votes each member has received, and which of them have been formally elected.

    When documenting the nomination process, the minutes must also indicate information about the nominating committee, particularly the name of the committee who presented the nominations. When taking down the number of votes per nominee, it is important to indicate who had tallied the votes. The declaration of elected officials must be included in the minutes as well.

    If these guidelines aren't followed, the group might encounter complications later on, causing confusion about the process and outcome of the election that had taken place during a particular meeting. For example, if your bylaws state that board members will serve a three-year term upon being elected. There are four board members in total, and to ensure the continuity of the operations, only two members will be elected at a time. This does not account for the possible vacancies or resignations of the board members.

    If the minutes of the meeting has not clearly documented the election of board members, the organization might not be able to keep track of whether or not the elected official will serve a full term, or just the remainder of the term.

- *Unfinished Businesses*

    Unfinished business pertains to items on the agenda that have not been resolved or discussed yet during the previous meeting. However, unfinished business may only be recorded on the minutes of the current meeting if it has been included in the agenda in the first place. If it has been included, then the secretary has to record the actions or decisions that have been made on that particular business.

- *New Business*

    For new business, the secretary must document who has made the motion in order to open the new item for discussion. It is not necessary to take note of who has seconded the motion. You may still do so, however, if that is the practice or preference of the group.

    When recording the main motions, it is important to write them in their final forms, meaning that all amendments, if any, have already been incorporated as well. The minutes should also indicate the actions taken for those motions—whether they have been adopted, lost, or postponed.

    On the other hand, motions that have been withdrawn do not have to be recorded in the minutes. If a motion is postponed but then withdrawn within the same meeting, the minutes should reflect the changes in the disposition of the given motion.

    Secondary motions that have been adopted are also part of the minutes of the meeting. For example, if a motion to take a recess has been adopted, the secretary should record the actual time that the members have taken their recess, as well as the exact time the meeting has been called back to order by the presiding officer.

- *Programs and Announcements*

    Near the end of the minutes, the secretary must indicate the following information:

    - The name of the program and its speaker, if ever there is one, should be recorded. There is no need, however, to summarize the points covered in the program by the speaker.

    - If there was any previous notice of motions given during the meeting, the secretary must take note of them. This includes the content of each motion as well. For instance, if a member has given a previous notice to amend a decision, the minutes should reflect this in the following manner:

        "Mr. Smith has given previous notice that in the succeeding meeting, he will amend the resolution to increase the duration of lunch break for all employees."

    - If the chair has made any important announcements during the meeting, the secretary must make note of the key parts of said announcement. For example, the chair may have announced that the next meeting will be conducted in a different venue and will begin earlier than the normal schedule. The minutes must reflect the exact location of the new venue, as well as the exact date and time of the next meeting. The secretary may also include the rationale or cause for this announcement so that the other members are aware of what brought about this change.

C. Meeting Adjournment and Signatures

The minutes should be ended by recording the details of when the meeting was formally adjourned. To signify that it is the end of the minutes, the individual who prepared the document should sign the document along with his or her title within the organization. This is typically the secretary, but there are certain meetings wherein the secretary cannot take part, whatever the reason may be. There are some organizations which require the presiding officer to sign the minutes, so you may want to consider applying the same practice within your organization.

D. Review, Approval of, and Corrections to the Minutes

As explained earlier, the minutes of the previous meeting must be read upon calling to order the current meeting. If there are opening ceremonies to go through, reading of the minutes may be postponed until the end of said activities.

To approve the minutes, there must be general consensus among the members that the contents are true and complete. If not, the members must make a motion to correct the minutes. This may be done regardless of how much time has lapsed since the previous meeting was conducted. Any corrections that must be made require a two-thirds majority vote, unless specified otherwise in the bylaws.

Once the minutes have been approved, the secretary will write "approved" on the dedicated field for this, usually at the very end of the document itself. This must be initialed by the secretary, and the date of signing must be indicated right beside it.

Final Version of the Minutes

In the early days of parliamentary procedures, secretaries were required to write the minutes by hand on pre-numbered, hardbound ledger books. With the advent of the computer and word processing software, organizations have since then utilized modern means of producing the minutes of the meeting. The challenge of using this method, however, is ensuring that every minutes is consecutively numbered and arranged in a logical order before being sent out for binding.

It is also important to remember that each subject warrants a separate paragraph. To further highlight this, some organizations employ the use of headers, especially for long discussions about a particular topic. Examples of typical headers include "Reports", "New Business", and "Unfinished Business".

Some secretaries utilize the wide page margins by writing brief summaries beside each paragraph. This would be helpful for those who want to locate a certain piece of information in the minutes of the meetings.

The organization has the freedom to choose how the final version of their minutes will appear. What matters more at this point is the assurance that the format will be applied consistently for all minutes in the future.

Chapter 9 – Frequently Asked Questions

When it comes to practicing and applying the principles and rules of the parliamentary procedures, individuals and organizations tend to have a common theme in terms of the queries and clarifications that arise. The majority of them are centered around the proper way of voting for or against a motion, laying out the agenda for a meeting, recording and disseminating the minutes of a meeting, and how to deal with problematic presiding officers.

If you are in a hurry to resolve your issues regarding the parliamentary procedures as applied to your organization, it's best to refer first to your bylaws and the other existing documents that govern your organization. More often than not, this topic has already been covered and explained in those materials. You may also consult the primary authority of your parliament, but it should be noted that bylaws and governing documents will always supersede and take precedence over the decisions or opinions of the parliamentary authority.

To further help you in resolving these matters, here are the commonly asked questions—grouped into their main topics for your convenience—about parliamentary procedures. Provided also below are the answers and suggestions as to how you can address them properly and in accordance with the prescriptions of Robert's Rules of Order.

Nominations and Elections

Question No. 1: *Should we require a second whenever a member nominates another member for any position? Is it needed before we can include that individual's name on the ballot?*

Answer: There is no need for a second on a nomination. As long as the person who has received the nomination is qualified for the position and eligible to serve the roles and responsibilities the position would entail, then his or her name can be written on the ballot.

Furthermore, according to Robert's Rules of Order, a nomination is not needed for someone to be included in the election. There should always be a space on the ballot where members can write down the name of a person they want to vote for. This does not mean though that everyone can be elected regardless of their qualifications and experience. The election committee still has to further evaluate this, hence the importance of going through the nomination process, instead of conducting a write-in election.

Question No. 2*: Is it specified anywhere in Robert's Rules of Order that an individual is not allowed to run for two different offices simultaneously. For example, there is one member in our organization who wants to run for both president and senator positions. There is another member who has received nominations for the presidency and vice-presidency. Are these incidences allowable in terms of the parliamentary procedures?*

Answer: The parliamentary procedures do not restrict the nomination of an individual for two offices. Typically, it is the bylaws of the organization that set and impose the said limitations to its members. In general, organizations do not allow their members to be elected and hold more than one office at a given time.

To address your concerns on this, you have to consider first the context of the situation that your organization is in. First, if the person who has been elected for two positions is present during the ceremony, he or she may be asked to choose which office he or she wants to serve. Whichever position is not chosen will go to the person with the second highest number of votes.

On the other hand, if the said person is not present when he or she has been elected to two offices, then the members who are present at that moment can decide or vote again to determine which of the two offices will be served by that person.

There is also a chance that the election process itself will solve the situation even without your intervention. More often than not, that person with two nominations will be elected to serve for one office only. In some cases, that person may not even win the election for either of the positions he or she has been nominated to.

It is better to wait for the results of the election, rather than block a nomination for a certain member of your organization. If that person has been elected for both offices, then you may proceed to conduct the specified procedures detailed above.

Question No. 3: *If the floor has already closed for nominations, is the president allowed to once again open the floor? If it is allowed, should another member put forward a motion to reopen the floor, or is the president able to do so out of his or her own will?*

Answer: As per the rules of parliamentary procedures, the floor may be opened again for nominations as long as it has gained the majority vote from the members. To initiate this, any member of the group can make the motion, including the chairperson. If there are no objections when the motion is made, then the chair can announce to the group that the floor is open once more for nominations. However, if there is even a single valid objection on the motion, then this has to be taken to a vote. Typically, a voice vote will suffice for this purpose.

According to Robert's Rules of Order, there are two main reasons why a group might want to reopen the floor during nominations and elections. First, it could be that, for whatever reason, the person who has gained the largest number of votes immediately declines to serve the office upon being elected. The second probable cause for this motion is that several rounds of votes have been done by the group, but none of the current nominees has been able to secure enough votes to be elected. In such cases, the group might want to add more names into the ballot so as to change and hopefully close the election process.

Question No. 4: *Following the bylaws of our university, the nominating committee is required to present a slate of nominees and gain the approval of the members of the board. How is "slate" defined in the parliamentary procedures? Is it the same as its literal definition as indicated in the dictionary, or is there more to it?*

Answer: In terms of parliamentary procedures, a slate of nominees means that there is only one nominee per vacancy in each office. For example, your organization has to elect a new president, vice president, and treasurer. A slate of nominees for those positions would mean that the nominating committee will be endorsing one name for each position. Following that principle, multiple slates require the committee to nominate more than one individual per office.

If taken from the point of parliamentary purposes, it is recommended for the nominating committee to choose only the best nominee out of all the probable candidates. Otherwise, requiring the committee to come up with options might lead them to consider even those that are not fully qualified or eligible to serve in those particular offices. Moreover, if the committee manages to secure equally qualified nominees, there can only be one winner between those two candidates. The other one would definitely be considered as the loser, and as such, he or she may decline to participate in the elections or accept nominations in the future.

This is in contrast with national elections wherein the people are always guaranteed to have at least two options to choose from. This is considered as a democratic process of selecting the leaders of the country. On the other hand, fostering that kind of competition between the members of an organization may be counterintuitive for the visions and missions of the group. The primary goal of electing officials in an organization is to select the best people for the job in order to further the achievement and progress of the group as a whole.

Again, there is no restriction stated in Robert's Rules of Order against the nomination of more than one individual for each office. That particular limitation has been removed so as to keep the nominating committee in check in terms of how objective they are with the selection process. If the members have valid proof that the committee is not serving its purpose well and objectively, then they are allowed to nominate other candidates that they consider as better choices than what has been presented by the committee.

Voting

Question No. 1: *There is someone in my organization who wishes to vote by proxy. Is there a minimum requirement for the proxy vote to be considered as valid?*

Answer: Your first point of consultation should be the statutes on proxy voting according to the state that your organization officially belongs to or has been incorporated in. In the event that the state allows organizations to take proxy votes for the type of organization that you have, then they will set out the rules for holding the proxy voting process and counting the individual or party who will be placing the vote instead.

Next, you must refer to the current bylaws of your organization. No member can permit or take a proxy vote if the bylaws do not allow it, unless the state statutes indicate otherwise. When it comes to the order of precedence, the state will always be more important than what is considered as valid or invalid in any organization belonging to the said state.

It should be noted by every party involved that Robert's Rules of Order does not recommend proxy voting for the majority of organizations. It is only advisable to be used for groups wherein the members hold a financial interest in the organization. This includes privately held corporations and neighborhood associations.

If the bylaws are yet to be written, you may ask yourself the following questions as guidance during the development phase of that particular document:

a. Is proxy voting really necessary for your organization?

   Check to ensure that it will not cause further complications in your meetings. Consider as well if, by allowing proxies, you will be inadvertently encouraging the habitual absence of the members. You should also evaluate the possible effects of banning proxy votes. In the worst-case scenario, you might be laying out the foundation for the organization to lose its democratic nature since the decision-making process is left only in the hands of those who are present during meetings.

b. Are proxies going to be allowed into the quorum? If yes, how are they going to be counted?

c. How much power is acceptable to be given to a proxy?

   When a proxy has the right to cast the vote for any motion according to his or her own view, then that refers to someone who has general authority. However, if the proxy is only allowed to vote in a certain way as stipulated in a written form, or if the proxy is only allowed vote in specific motions, then that individual has limited authority.

d. Who will be assigned to validate the authenticity and powers of the proxy?

e. How does the procedure for counting the proxy votes differ from the votes given by present members?

f. How long is the validity of the proxy? Is it valid only for one meeting? Or does the proxy last for a certain period of time?

g. Can the members revoke their proxies in the middle of a meeting?

When you are writing the section of your bylaws pertaining to proxy votes, you have to keep in mind the main purpose of why your organization holds meetings in the first place. Generally, the objective of the meeting is to provide a venue wherein members can interact personally while discussing or debating a certain matter. Meetings should also be concluded with an agreement by the whole group as to how they will act on, or decide, regarding the said matter.

Sometimes, members might have a pre-determined resolution or opinion in their minds even before attending the meeting. However, while listening to their peers, officers, or subordinates during the meeting, they may still change their views and vote in an entirely different manner. If a proxy would be allowed to take the place of certain members, then this aspect of the process would no longer happen.

Question No. 2: *How can we properly break a tie between two nominees for an officer position? Is the president allowed to decide who should win by casting a tie-breaking vote? If that is permissible, then should the tie-breaking vote be taken immediately after the votes have been counted, or only after the meeting has resumed and the members have given their opinions regarding this matter?*

Answer: As stated in Robert's Rules of Order, the president should always vote, along with the other members, using the ballot system. Since the president has voted already, he or she is not allowed to vote once more.

There is a proper way of handling a tie during an election, according to the parliamentary procedures. First, the president must announce that there has been a tie between two nominees. Then, the president will instruct the members to do another round of voting until one of the nominees has gained more votes than the other.

Certain organizations, however, do allow the president to break the tie during an election, but they still follow the democratic principle of making all votes have an equal amount of power. For them, the president is still required to vote in a ballot, but the vote will not be counted along with those of the members. When a tie has been determined, the president will then reveal his or her vote as stated in the ballot, thereby breaking the tie. The announcement of the results will be done only when the president's vote has been counted as well.

Question No. 3: *During a roll call vote, is there a certain order of members that must be followed? Who should go first, and who should go last? Is the order the same for every motion, or does it change depending on the motion?*

Answer: According to the parliamentary procedures, the correct order is alphabetical, excluding the president's name which must only be read last when his or her vote will affect the final resolution.

The members have four ways to respond when their names have been read by the secretary. A member who agrees with the motion has to say "yes", while those in opposition have to say "no." If the member does not wish to participate in the vote, then he or she will have to express this by saying "abstain" or "present", indicating that even though that particular member is present, he or she will not be voting for or against a certain resolution. The fourth way to respond is by saying "pass", indicating that the member has not yet made up his or her mind yet regarding the vote. Those who avail this option will be given more time to think, but they can only do this once per voting session.

Upon stating one's vote, the secretary is required to repeat the statement before recording it next to the respective member's name on the tally sheet or board. After everyone has given their votes, the president will ask if the vote is final or not. Everyone is permitted to change their votes at this point, provided that the secretary has not yet begun the final tally count, and that no announcement has been made yet by the president about the final result of the vote.

After all votes have been counted, the secretary shall state the total number of votes for each side, as well the total number of members who have completely abstained from the vote. The president will then announce the result of the votes, and if the motion will be carried forward or if the motion has been lost.

Question No. 4: *The members of our organization are debating on the value and effect of abstaining from a vote. Many believe that choosing this option during a vote indicates that the individual is actually against the motion. Are there any rules to guide the handling of abstainers? Do we have an alternative way of handling those who wish to abstain from the vote?*

Answer: To resolve this, you must determine first how your organization defines a majority vote. In the case that your bylaws have already covered this, then there are different ways for how you can interpret the stipulations pertaining to abstainers.

If your organization's rules indicate that all motions must be carried forward only through a majority vote, then that "majority" refers to all members who have cast their votes. An abstain vote tells you then that the person is choosing not to vote at all, and therefore their vote does not count for either of the two opposing sides.

On the other hand, if your bylaws state that the motion must be agreed upon by the "majority of those present" or the "majority of the entire assembly", then an abstain vote will skew the results of the vote towards the "no" side.

To illustrate this, in the event that a group of ten has decided to take a vote, wherein the votes of the majority of everyone present during the meeting will determine the fate of the resolution. Upon tallying the results, the president announces that four members have voted "yes", three members have voted "no", and three members have chosen to abstain from the vote. Given the rules governing this particular group, the resolution, in this case, has been defeated.

It may sound like a simple matter, but there are certain points to this aspect of voting that must be taken into consideration if your organization is still deciding on how to define the majority vote. In large organizations wherein there is high number of voting members, counting the votes of the participants is completely fine. On the other hand, when there are only a few voting members, demanding the majority vote of the entire group will prevent the likelihood of only a subset of the group from pushing their agenda when more members are either against or undecided about a certain motion. By agreeing to this rule, you are avoiding the occurrence of controversies or conflicts that may arise among the group members.

Question No. 5: During our last meeting, one member arrived late due to a personal matter that she had to attend to. We were in the middle of taking votes, but in consideration to her, the process was paused to get her up to speed with what the motion was all about, and how the discussion went earlier. After around twenty minutes of recapping the activities she had missed, the member casted her vote. Only then did the voting process resume. During the latter part of the meeting, after the results had already been announced, some members voiced their concerns about the incident. Apparently, the way it was handled caused confusion among them, and some even lost track of where the meeting was heading. How do we properly handle such incidents, in case this happens again in the future?

Answer: According to Robert's Rules of Order, there should be no unnecessary interruption while taking the votes of the members. Interruptions to a vote can be allowed only when the secretary has not yet started taking the votes of each member. Otherwise, the group should continue taking the votes until the process has been completed.

In the situation described above, the interruption caused by the one tardy member of the group is simply unacceptable. She knew of the schedule and agenda of the meeting, but she still chose to arrive late for the meeting without prior advisement to any member of the group. Therefore, the other members are not obliged to stop their activities and explain to her what had transpired while she was absent. In the case that a certain member wishes to do so, then the explanation can be given while the votes are being tallied.

The President

Question No. 1: *Does the president have the authority to select the issues and motions that will be discussed and decided upon by the other members of the board?*

Answer: According to Robert's Rules of Order, the president has no power to filter out the motions and business that will be presented to the board, unless the bylaws of your organization state otherwise. If there are such rules, then the president would have the authority to rule out motions based on how the intent, purpose, or content of a certain motion conflicts with specific parts of the bylaws, or government laws at the national, state, or local level.

The president may express his or her objection about the motion, however. This does not mean though that such an objection will prevent the motion from being presented to the board. The objection will be noted by the group and will be taken into consideration when the board decides to vote upon the given motion.

Question No. 2: *There is one member in our organization that dislikes our current president. He has already caused several disruptions in our meetings and elections, causing us to waste time and energy on unnecessary discussions and votes. Is there any way to prevent him from doing this again?*

Answer: Since your president has been elected through the majority vote of your members, he or she deserves the full support of the organization regardless of the personal views of the members before and during the election process. The situation described above is a common example of an issue that poses a challenge to the democratic nature of your organization. In particular, that disruptive member is ignoring the requirement for every member to comply with the rules of the majority, even if he had not voted as part of the majority.

Robert's Rules of Order promotes the diplomatic and objective resolution of all matters, including personal issues between members and the elected officials. Avoid confronting him or imposing penalties on him right off the bat. The best way to handle this is to invite him for a one-on-one talk wherein you could point out the detrimental effects of his words and behaviors to the organization as a whole, instead of just their effects on the president.

Once he has acknowledged your point, you may then proceed to encourage him to become more cooperative and supportive of the president. Remind him that it is best to keep an open mind instead of reacting negatively and jumping to conclusions.

Question No. 3: *For some unspecified reason, our president does not want to include an item, as requested by some of the members, to the agenda of the meeting. The agenda also has* no provisions for the old or new businesses, as well as for the unfinished businesses. Our organization does not practice approving the agenda at the start of the session itself. Is it okay for me to ask for an approval of the agenda? Can I also make a motion for an item to be added to the agenda?

Answer: As indicated in Robert's Rules of Order, any member of the group is allowed to bring items to the floor in case the president has not included them in the original agenda. The main purpose of an agenda is to maintain the order of the meeting and keep everyone on track with the important matters that need to be discussed or voted upon by the group. This means that a meeting's agenda is not personal in nature, and therefore, the president cannot set an agenda that is solely based on what he or she thinks is significant or urgent.

The president has not been elected to that position in order to force his or her will upon the members of the organization. Instead, the president is selected for his or her capabilities in leading the members. For meetings and other assembly, his or her main priority should be to ensure the fairness and objectivity of the meeting itself.

The parliamentary procedures have been quite specific on what should be included in a meeting's agenda. If there are any pending matters that should be discussed, or decisions that must be made during the meeting, those items have to be included in the agenda under the category of "unfinished business". If you are not sure of the existence of such items, you may refer to the minutes of the previous meetings. In fact, to avoid overlooking any unfinished business, the secretary is required to read the minutes of the previous meeting out loud at the start of the current meeting.

In the case that both the president and the secretary failed to include unfinished business on the agenda, any member can put forward a parliamentary inquiry regarding this matter. During that exchange, the member can ask for a clarification as to why the item was not included, and when the said item will be discussed, if not during the current meeting. By doing so, you are politely bringing the attention of the whole group to the item that has been overlooked.

There are some instances wherein the exclusion might not be deliberate. The president may be uninformed about the significance or urgency of that particular item. If that is the case, then, in your parliamentary enquiry, you may explain this to him or her. However, if they purposely skipped over an item of unfinished business, then you may be dealing with a tyrant president.

To handle a tyrant president, you must follow the process for bringing up unfinished business that has been left out of the agenda. You may also ask why there is no new business included in the agenda. From there, you can request for the items to be added to the agenda. If the president once again refuses to do so, then you have to make a formal motion to add the unfinished or new businesses to the agenda of the meeting. That motion must be seconded and must gain a majority vote before it can be adopted.

Should the president continue to ignore the majority rule, then you may now raise a point of order. If that point of order has been ignored once more, you have to make another motion about the inclusion of said items into the agenda. Like before, you need to secure a second before it can be voted upon. However, this time, the motion will be presented to the board, thereby making the motion a point for the discussion and vote of the board members.

Any time that the president shows signs of tyranny, the members can follow this procedure to secure the place of said items on the agenda. However, it is important to go through each of the steps for this to be considered as valid.

Meetings

Question No. 1: *Some members of the board have a tendency to add items to the agenda during the meeting itself. How can we prevent them from doing so, and how can we stop someone without sounding too harsh?*

Answer: Setting the agenda of the meeting prior to the activity itself is highly recommended. By doing so, your group will be able to maintain the order and keep everyone on track with the purpose and direction of the meeting. Important business that must be discussed would also be settled faster and more effectively.

If a certain matter only requires the members to be notified of its existence, then it should not be added to an already established agenda. However, if it is deemed as urgent, then the addition of the said item must be decided upon by a majority vote from at least two-thirds of the group.

If no agenda had been set at the start of the meeting, then any member of the group is allowed to add items for discussion. This can be initiated by one member making a motion when the presiding officer calls for any new business that must be addressed.

It is important to note, however, that the agenda of the meeting should remain flexible enough so that members can bring up urgent matters prior to the assembly. The timing is key for sending out the agenda, since everyone should be notified about the purpose of the meeting—hence, the requirement for the addition to be made before the meeting.

Another important thing to keep in mind is that adopting the agenda is not a means of limiting the ideas of any member of the group. It is just a tool to maintain the order and keep everyone objective during the meeting. Furthermore, the president is not allowed to impose agenda items on the rest of the group. According to parliamentary procedures, one of the primary objectives of leaders is to protect the rights of the members during meetings. This means that they must ensure that the wishes of the members are carried out, and that ideas can be brought forward so that the group can fully evaluate and discuss them in a systematic manner.

Question No. 2: *Can non-elected members join a board meeting if they have valid concerns that must be discussed and decided upon immediately? Our bylaws state that non-members are not allowed to attend meetings, unless their invitation has been recommended by a member of the group, and duly approved by the president. Does this rule apply to our query about board meetings as well?*

Answer: According to Robert's Rules of Order, attendance to board meetings is normally exclusive to the elected members of the board. This is what practitioners refer to as an "executive session" of the board.

If regular members of an organization do have issues that they wish to bring to the attention of the board members, there are various ways to achieve such an objective. First, the members can request for a hearing so that they can present their case to the board. Once they are done, the board shall assure them that the issues have been heard, and a decision regarding the presented issues will be made known to everyone within a specified timeframe. It is then customary to ask in a polite manner, or escort gracefully the regular members, out of the room so that the board can proceed with their agenda.

The other way of informing the board of the issues being faced by the members is through a letter. All necessary information about the matters shall be put into writing by the concerned individuals. This will be then sent to the board so that they can include the contents of the letter in the agenda of their next board meeting.

There are some cases when members may simply be feeling curious about what goes on during a board meeting. They do not really have pressing matters that must be presented to, or decided upon, by the board. In such instances, these members must be reminded that board meetings are closed from the rest of the group. Pertinent information will be shared with them during the next full assembly meeting through the board's reports.

Question No. 3: *Is the chairperson of a committee allowed to make a motion during a meeting with the other committee members?*

Answer: As the head of a given committee, the chair is permitted to make a motion, join the debate about a motion, and submit his or her own vote regarding a certain motion. However, this only applies to a committee that is made up of no more than twelve members.

Beyond this size, the committee is considered to be a public body. In this case, the chair's privileges and responsibilities become more similar to those of the presiding officer that leads meetings. Because of this, the chair would no longer be allowed to make a motion, or debate about a motion. The only time a chair would be allowed to formally vote is when it is done through a ballot, or in the case that a tie between two opposing sides has to be broken.

Question No. 4: *If a particular member of the board has been found, or has personally declared, to have a significant conflict of interest about a certain topic, should that individual leave the meeting while the said topic is being covered or voted upon by the group?*

Answer: Before referring to the parliamentary procedures' ruling on this, you need to define first the probable conflicts of interest that a member might encounter with regard to the topics that are going to be discussed during a board meeting. In general, conflicts of interest originate from the personal motives of a certain member, especially when it comes to the financial aspects of the organization. In addition, it can only be a conflict of interest if said interest is not common among the other members of the board, or the organization as a whole.

As a general rule, a member with an identified conflict of interest regarding a particular topic should not be allowed to join the discussion or submit their vote on the topic. However, there is no specific rule about whether or not that person has to leave the room where the meeting is being held. Therefore, the decision on this matter is left to the agreement of the members, as stated in the group's bylaws, on how to handle situations like this.

Since the said person is not allowed to vote, he or she will also no longer be counted in the quorum. In the event that the person's presence is required in the quorum, then he or she will still be allowed to attend, but no voting on any issue can take place.

Minutes of the Meeting

Question No. 1: *Is there a proper format for the minutes of the meeting that must be followed? What details should be included in the minutes? Is there any piece of information that the secretary may leave out of the minutes? Should I be mindful of any legal requirements whenever I am assigned to take the minutes of the meeting?*

Answer: Even though Robert's Rules of Order does not provide a specific template for the minutes, it does provide a detailed description of its purpose and structure. In general, the minutes are a documentation of what has transpired during a meeting, not merely what has been said by the facilitator and attendees. However, if an organization chooses to publish its minutes to the general public, then a tape recorder would be necessary since every exchange and declaration must be included.

For the legal requirements related to the minutes of the meeting, you should refer your inquiries to the Secretary of State assigned to the state where your organization or company has been incorporated. This office can provide you the details and guidelines that you must follow in order to ensure the legality of your minutes. This is important since all minutes of the meeting are considered a legal document of the organization or company. In fact, when in court, a judge and jury would refer to the minutes when it comes to making a decision about a related case.

Aside from the significant details of the meeting, it can be helpful to document background information as well. This can help to serve as rationale behind a decision.

Question No. 2: *Given the new forms of technology and products available nowadays, are there new prescribed ways to properly bind the minutes of the meeting?*

Answer: The best way to bind the minutes of the meeting is through the use of the secretary's book. This product is made up of a hardcover with 150 blank pages inside it. It is available in major office supply stores and typically costs about $75.00 each. Even though the initial purchase is high compared to other similar products, the secretary's book is refillable. This means that once you have consumed the first 150 pages included in the set, you can purchase only the paper instead.

To use the secretary's book, you need to first record the contents of the minutes of the meeting using your computer. Once you have entered in every piece of information, you need to take out the same number of blank pages from the secretary's book as the number of pages to be printed as indicated in your preferred word processing application.

Using any type of printer, use the blank pages when printing out the minutes of the meeting. Finally, put back the printed minutes into the secretary's book. Repeat this process until you have used up your blank pages, or when you wish to bind the minutes.

Nowadays, there are various printing shops that offer a binding service for the secretary's book. All you have to do is bring the minutes that need to be bound to a shop for binding and labeling. Depending on the shop's capabilities, you can get the bound minutes of the meeting within the same day of your order.

Motions

Question No. 1: *Should a resolution have a second?*

Answer: A resolution is simply the formal manner of stating a main motion. Therefore, the rules for main motions apply to resolutions as well. If only one member proposes a main motion, there should be another member who will say that he or she seconds the motion. On the other hand, if a committee comprised of more than one voting member proposes a main motion, there is no need to second the motion anymore.

Question No. 2: *Can a rejected motion be brought up and voted upon again by the members? If this is not typically possible, what situations can serve as a means of creating an exception to the rule?*

Answer: According to Robert's Rules of Order, any motion that has already been defeated is not allowed to be brought up again within the same meeting, unless certain conditions have been met, or are applicable to the situation.

First, if a member from the side that garnered the majority vote has motioned for the group to reconsider the vote, another round of voting will take place once the motion is seconded and approved. Second, if time or specific circumstances have changed how the motion can be regarded by the members, then the motion can be put up for voting once more.

If neither of the said conditions apply to your case, then the defeated motion may only be brought up again upon the next scheduled meeting of the group. This action is formally referred to as renewing the motion.

Conclusion

Thanks for taking the time to read this book on Robert's Rules of Order.

You should now have a good understanding of parliamentary procedures, and how to implement Robert's Rules in to your own organization.

Remember, the full implementation of Robert's Rules can take time, but it is well worth it. Through the successful use of Robert's Rules, you will experience better, more productive meetings, and happier members of your organization.

Thanks again for choosing this book, I hope you have found it to be helpful!

www.ingramcontent.com/pod-product-compliance
Lightning Source LLC
LaVergne TN
LVHW011722060526
838200LV00051B/2998